NO PRESSURE STEAM COOKING

STEAM YOUR WAY TO SKINNY BEAUTIFUL SUCCESS!

D0514552

BY ROBERT W. ZINKHON

PHOTOGRAPHY BY GRACE KENNAN WARNECKE

Drawings by Michael Pearce
Design by Jane Walsh
Editor/Food Consultant Joy Windle

ISBN 0-912738-12-X
Library of Congress No. 77-89308
Printed in the United States of America
Copyright© 1978 Robert W. Zinkhon
Published by Taylor & Ng
P.O. Box 200
Brisbane, California 94005
    All Rights Reserved
    First Edition, Fifth Printing
Distributed by Random House, Inc.
and in Canada by Random House of Canada, Ltd.
ISBN 0-394-73564-1

The Author

Robert Zinkhon claims he was lured into writing a book about steam cooking by Win Ng and Spaulding Taylor, founding fathers of Taylor & Ng, on whose board of directors Zinkhon has been since the firm's inception.

He heads his own public relations and advertising firm, Robert Zinkhon Communications, in San Francisco. His clients do not include restaurants, food products or anything related to eating and cooking, he hastens to point out.

A bachelor, he was forced to learn self-defense in the kitchen. He considers his own, infrequent cooking interesting, but does not expect to significantly advance culinary frontiers.

Committed to write the book, Zinkhon locked himself in the steamy, murky depths of his kitchen, and became, he alleges, the world's foremost authority on steam cooking. He would create fascinating recipes at his typewriter, get up full steam and experiment to see if his plans would work. Some did, indeed. He believes his expertise will go unchallenged until someone else faces the misty seclusion of a sauna-like apartment for several months.

Zinkhon, who has traveled extensively, is intrigued with the cuisines of every country he visits, and has found that many noted dishes adapt readily to the steampot. Also a painter, he thinks the kitchen offers opportunities as creative as the canvas, and that each dish should be a handsome still life.

He wrote this book, he says, for those who like to entertain well, yet painlessly, and who enjoy wallowing in praise about their achievements. He hopes the book will help you steam your way to skinny, beautiful, success in the kitchen.

The Photographer

Born in Riga, Latvia, as the daughter of former Ambassador George F. Kennan and his Norwegian wife, Annelise, Grace Kennan Warnecke grew up in both Europe and the United States. She has had a life-long interest in food, but is fairly new to photography. Her work as a free lance writer led her to the field of photo-journalism. She studied photography at the Corcoran School of Art in Washington, D.C. and also at the San Francisco Art Institute. Her first published photograph was of President Ford at the moment of the attempted assassination by Sara Jane Moore which appeared in Time Magazine. "From that moment on, people assumed I was a professional photographer, so I became one," she said.

Grace Warnecke was official photographer for the San Francisco Twin Bicentennial. Her first photography show of authors was at Minerva's Owl Bookstore in San Francisco and her most recent one-woman show, entitled "Familiar Faces," was displayed at the Van Doren Gallery in San Francisco in 1977. She works as a photographer and writer in San Francisco, where she lives with her three children, Charles, Adair and Kevin.

The Editor/ Food Consultant

Joy Windle, whose lifetime avocation has been cooking, became a professional a few years ago when she and a partner formed the San Francisco catering company, Joie de Vivre. They are especially noted for brilliant French cuisine and superb presentation.

A graduate of Vassar College, she has lived in England and has

traveled extensively in Europe. Great food and great books have always been a part of her life, for her mother is an oustanding cook, her father, a rare book dealer.

A native of New York, she has lived in San Francisco for six years. During this time she has also studied interior design at the Rudolph Schaeffer School.

Joy Windle's remarkable knowledge of food and syntax have been of enormous value to the author, and no little comfort to the publisher.

CONTENTS

1 DAMN THE TORPEDOES... introduction

5 STEAMWARE equipment

7 GETTING UP STEAM the basic liquids

9 STEAMING THROUGH EUROPE AND NORTH AFRICA meats and one-pot meals

19 SEAFOOD STEAM TRIPS IN SAN FRANCISCO

27 VAPORS, VEGETABLES AND VICTORIES

51 STEAMY FRUIT FRONTIERS

61 TASTEFUL, WELLBREAD STEAMING bread, rolls and muffins

65 STANLEY STEAMER'S HOLIDAY DINNER

69 THE MISTY ASSIGNATION DINNER FOR TWO

73 SAUCES: HOW TO TOP YOUR OWN COOKING

77 DESSERTS: PUDDING THEM IN THE STEAMPOT

DAMN THE TORPEDOES...

It steams to me . . .

Steaming may well be the most civilized method of cooking.

Food that has been steamed looks better, tastes better, and indeed, *is* better for you. It is fresher, greener, yellower, purpler or whatever color it was intended to be. It's the slimmer, trimmer method of cooking. It's easier. It's versatile. And, in the case of meats, it's more economical.

Steamed foods have style. They open new culinary vistas. They can be simple, or make important gastronomic statements. They are as essential to down-home, country cooking as to grande cuisine.

Steamed foods certainly have far more nutritional value than those cooked almost any other way. Clearly, when we boil vegetables or fruits, a lot of the vitamins and other food value go down the drain with the water they have been cooked in. Steaming keeps the flavor and the healthful elements right where they belong.

When steaming meats and fowl, much of the fat is rendered and drips into the cooking liquid below, continuing to add flavor, but

not as many calories and cholesterol problems. So, not only do we stay healthier, we are staying trimmer and slimmer, too.

Although this book is in no sense a diet special, nor does it offer the much-touted cuisine minceur, the recipes and menus featured are essentially simple, uncluttered with rich sauces, and perfectly suited to the skinny, beautiful and vigorous lives most of us wish to live today.

Now let's understand one thing right away. Steam cooking has nothing to do with "steam tables", a necessary evil used by hotel banquet kitchens, certain restaurants, hospitals and army mess halls. The steam table is designed to keep cooked foods warm, but the result is soggy and depressing by the time they are served.

Practically any food can be steamed, although most cooks rest their case with a few green vegetables. Well, there is an exciting new frontier in your kitchen. With me as your guide, you're going to enter a misty new world of steamed surprises. There will be tender, succulent ribs, spicy

Left to right:
Spaulding Taylor, Philippe Henry, Charlotte Mailliard

1

FULL STEAM AHEAD!

sausages, delicious briskets of beef, chicken, hams, and corned beef. We'll steam apples and pears, peaches and grapes, pots de crème à la vanille. We'll solve many mysteries of the egg, be they shirred, scrambled, hard or soft-steamed. We'll steam salmon, oysters, crab and shrimp. We'll even invade the baker's domain and steam bread, rolls and cake!

Especially valuable will be the meals-in-one-pot with which we will deal. Here we have been inspired by the international classics: Italian bollito misto. French pot au feu. Alsatian choucroute garnie. Moroccan couscous. Irish corned beef and cabbage. Spanish paella. All, needless to say, we shall steam.

Steamed foods are also interesting when they are counterpointed with other textures, other aromas and other colors. What, after all, can equal a standing rib roast, a young leg of lamb or a rich ham roasting in all its juices and filling the whole apartment or house with delectable aromas? Or chops broiling, chicken frying or fish grilling?

In every case, crisply fresh steamed vegetables are abso-lutely essential on the menu, and nothing could be better for a finale than a steamed apple or pear with chopped nuts, heavy cream, a good liqueur and a dusting of nutmeg.

The multi-rack steamer offers a marvelous convenience, for you can cook so many items at the same time and in the same pot. Further, the steampot is the easiest cooking utensil to clean. There are never caked or burned foods to scrape and scrub, and never a need to soak a pot or pan.

Steam cooking is simplicity itself. Anyone can do it. It is valuable for large or small families, for couples, and for singles, whatever age or lifestyle.

Because cooking interests me more as a creative experience than for the mere preparation of food to serve and eat, we'll talk about the challenges and opportunities steam cooking affords. We'll be especially concerned with appearance and presentation.

In a later chapter this book offers the bachelor, male or female, a specific special-occasion menu, The Assignation Dinner for Two.

Join me in the steamy side of life.

Left to right: Simon Lowinsky, Charlotte Mailliard, Peter Culley, Spaulding Taylor, Del Simmons, Philippe Henry.

STEAMWARE

Equipment

Fortunately, you really do not need fancy equipment to be a good steam chef. For years I have steamed vegetables in a colander or large strainer over a pot of boiling water. I have a floppy wire basket that apparently has some mysterious purpose unknown to me, but I have used that for steaming, too.

A widely used little steamer is the French gadget that folds and unfolds like flower petals. This is also used over a pot of boiling water. Another famous steamer is the tall cylinder-like pot with a perforated insert that holds asparagus vertically.

Still another steamer is a ceramic or stoneware pot that resembles a flat bowl with a chimney in the center. This is placed over a pot of boiling water, and instead of the steam rushing through perforations, it comes up the chimney and circulates within the tightly-lidded bowl. A similar pot has been used by the Chinese for centuries.

A recent introduction by small appliance manufacturers is an electric steamer that features both perforated racks and a covered dish, where rice, stewed tomatoes, applesauce or other foods of this consistency can be cooked. While it does have the advantages of any electrical appliance, there are also overtones of a mini steam table. It just doesn't steam like old times to me.

The Chinese and Japanese also use bamboo steamer racks over water boiling in a wok with a lid. But, even without these items, you can quite simply prop a bowl or plate of food on empty tin cans or heat-proof jelly jars and steam a highly successful dish.

But for no pressure steam cooking, I prefer an aluminum steam pot, available in ten-inch or twelve-inch diameters. There are four easy pieces: a large bottom pan (the ten-inch holds four quarts of liquid, the twelve-inch holds six quarts), two perforated racks, and a tight-fitting cover.

Happily, additional racks are available, and I use as many as four. Since the steampot is made of aluminum (only the handle on the lid is wood), it is easily washed and easily stored.

I do not worry about temperatures when using the steampot. Just put it on the stove, heat water to boiling, and place the racks on the steamer. Your prime concern is timing, and understanding that foods on the first rack over the water get more heat than those above. For example, I may steam potatoes on the first level for twenty-five minutes, but steam the snow peas on the fourth level for three minutes. When cooking meats that require a few hours, you don't need furiously boiling water. Just let it perk enough to generate a good amount of steam.

Times suggested in this book are a reasonable guide, yet I find variations in the foods themselves as well as the number of people for whom you are cooking require periodic probing with a fork, or slicing into the meats to find out what actually is happening. Remember, of course, that every time you open the lid and release steam, you'll have to add a bit more cooking time.

GETTING UP STEAM

The Basic Liquids

Fill the pot at least two-thirds full of liquid, primarily because you don't want to worry about it boiling away. If you're steaming meat for more than an hour, check at least once an hour to see if you should add more liquid.

The easiest, simplest, most effective liquid in general is water. But, some dishes are superb if steamed in beer, wine or champagne. Choucroute garnie, the wonderful Alsatian dish of sauerkraut, sausages, ham, spareribs and bacon, for example, is wonderful steamed in beer or champagne. Let your mood and your pocketbook decide.

Instead of using plain water, when steaming meats and vegetables, I sometimes add salt and lemon juice or vinegar as well, along with peppercorns and whole cloves of garlic. For sturdy meals-in-one-pot, stews, chicken and most meats, marvelously rich flavors are gained by adding chopped carrots, onions, leeks, celery, parsley, bay leaves and other fresh or dried herbs either to the steaming liquid or on the rack with the meat. Another possibility is to add beef or chicken bouillon freshly made, frozen, canned or in cubes. Most fresh bones add great flavor, too.

If you're lucky and have an herb garden, or can get fresh herbs at your local market, they are an important plus in your stock, as well as directly on the meats and vegetables. I've got big pots of them growing on my deck, and toss generous handfuls of oregano, thyme, fresh bay, rosemary, basil and dill into the steam stock. If you plan to use it for soup or as a marinade, tie cloth around it to create a bouquet garni.

A rule of thumb. Make the steaming liquid far stronger than you would if the foods were boiling in it, for obviously the flavor will be gently imparted to the steaming foods. Therefore, the steam stock can be sharper, tarter, more vinegary, saltier, more heavily garlicked.

There are times when you may have one of the meats in the actual liquid itself, while other foods are stacked in the upper racks. For the bollito misto dinner in this book, you'll note that the corned beef is submerged in the liquid, while the chicken, brisket and sausages are in the racks.

Here is your chance to cut loose and be creative. Come up with interesting flavor combinations for the steam liquid. I don't see how you can fail.

STEAMING THROUGH EUROPE AND NORTH AFRICA

Meats and One Pot Meals

Every culture and almost every country seems to have at least one noted and altogether delicious meal in one pot that is boiled or stewed. We will deal with several of the best known and most popular of these tasty dishes, but we shall not boil, stew, simmer, submerge or drown ours. Naturally, we shall steam them.

From Italy we'll borrow the tempting bollito misto, which means boiled mixture of meats and vegetables and spicy, aromatic herbs. From France, we'll present our own pot au feu and poule au pot, gusty, simple dinners that can be served soup-like in a bowl, or on a plate using the juices as sauce or gravy.

From Alsace, we'll create a monumental choucroute garnie, that delicious concoction of meats and sauerkraut that is titillated with juniper berries or a healthy slug of good gin. Closer to home, Irish corned beef and cabbage is a less sophisticated, but no less delicious variation on the theme of meat and cabbage. It steams beautifully, and the cabbage always remains crisp.

From Spain—paella, a dish as pleasing to the artist's palette as to the epicure's palate. Yellow saffron rice, pink prawns, golden chicken, bright green peas, red pimento, and much more. Finally, from North Africa, we'll steam up a couscous every bit as good as the first one I ever tasted in Tunis some years ago.

A Steamer's Answer to Bollito Misto (Italian)

It is unlikely that any Italian cook, at home or in a restaurant, would give you the same recipe for bollito misto, and chances are, their own will vary depending upon what seemed most interesting that day at the market. But the emphasis is always the same, featuring several meats and chicken cooked together, with vegetables used primarily for flavoring rather than for serving.

Popular ingredients include beef tongue, garlic-flavored pork sausages, rump roasts, leg of veal, stewing chicken, ham and brisket of beef. Actually, almost any of the less expensive cuts of meat are ideal, for they require long, slow cooking, have superb flavor, and all add agreeable nuances of taste to one another.

We are offering a variation that rates ten on a scale of ten. I don't know what the Italians would think, but I used corned beef as the prime meat. With this I steamed brisket of beef, Polish garlic sausage and chicken. The corned beef seemed to trigger a flavor explosion that was memorable.

Bollito Misto

Serves six

2½ pounds corned beef
2 pounds brisket of beef
1 pound Polish garlic sausage
2 pounds chicken
3 onions, chopped
3 carrots, chopped
3 celery stalks and leaves,
    chopped
5 garlic cloves
12 peppercorns
Handful of parsley
Handful of fresh herbs—thyme,
    oregano, savory, tarragon and
    bay. Or, if dried, ½ teaspoon
    of each plus 1 bay leaf.
1 lemon, chopped
½ cup vinegar

To 4 quarts of water add the
vegetables, peppercorns, garlic,
lemon, vinegar, and herbs. Add
corned beef. Bring to a boil, then
reduce heat and simmer for three
hours. You'll note that this is one
of the few times we actually boil,
rather than steam a meat. The
reason is that we need every layer
of the steamer, and the corned
beef flavor steams effectively
through the other meats when it is
actually part of the steam liquid.

After one hour, add the brisket
of beef to the first rack. After
another hour, add the Polish sausage to the second rack. In thirty
minutes add the whole chicken

to the top rack and steam everything for thirty more minutes.

Presentation Transfer meats to
a carving board to drain and to
firm up for easier cutting. Strain
the steam liquid, toss in a handful
of pasta, cook until it is barely
al dente, and serve as soup for
the first course.

Peel the sausage. Arrange meats
neatly on a heated platter. Garnish generously with watercress,
and carve at the table. Serve with
a big, tangy green salad, crunchy
bread sticks and sweet butter, and
some gutsy red wine. To accompany the meats, offer choices
of mustard sour cream sauce,
some Dijon mustard, hot English
mustard, and no-nonsense
horseradish.

Mustard Sour Cream Sauce

1 cup sour cream
4 tablespoons Dijon style mustard
2 tablespoons lemon juice
Salt and freshly ground pepper to
    taste
2 tablespoons chopped chives

Whisk ingredients together; garnish with chopped chives.

Pot au Feu and Poule au Pot (French)

The French pot au feu is another
of those highly personalized,
international-in-scope, stewed,
boiled, braised or baked dinners.
As you know, ours will be
steamed. It is a no-nonsense, reli-
able, attractive meal-in-one-pot,
as welcome at a chic dinner party
on Nob Hill as at a down-home
bachelor buffet.

Elegant though it may be, the
price is right, for with our steaming methods, the less expensive
cuts of meat are not a com-
promise, they are a must. It would
be sinful to steam a New York
steak, and moreover, the flavor
would not be as superb as that of
the beef chuck shoulder pot roast
we'll use in this pot au feu.

Perhaps this should be Zinkhon's
rule (just invented): as basic tenderness of meat increases, flavor
decreases. Think now. Filet is
tender, melt-in-the-mouth, but
cannot touch many other steak
cuts for flavor. In fact, the finest
flavor of all is found in flank steak.
This is so tough that it is ordinarily
marinated first, then grilled,
carved on the extreme diagonal,
and, let us give thanks,
transformed into the tastiest steak
of all.

So, if you think you must spend

two or three times more money for great meat, you are wrong. Don't be intimidated. Steam your way to skinny, successful popularity! Economically. And, blessedly, simply.

Pot au Feu

Serves six

4 pounds boneless beef chuck shoulder pot roast (Variations: brisket of beef, short ribs, neck pot roast)
1 bottle good red Burgundy
2 onions, chopped
2 stalks of celery with leaves
4 cloves garlic, chopped
1 tablespoon salt
12 or so peppercorns
3 bay leaves
Handful of parsley
Handful of fresh herbs: thyme, oregano, savory, tarragon. If not available, use ¼ teaspoon each of dried herbs.
8 beef or chicken bouillon cubes
1 quart water
6 medium carrots, halved vertically
6 medium peeled potatoes, halved vertically
3 onions, halved horizontally
1 medium head of cabbage, cut in wedges
6 fresh young parsnips or turnips, if available.

Add wine, onions, celery, garlic, salt, pepper, herbs and bouillon cubes to water, bring to a boil, and reduce heat to a steamy simmer. Thoroughly brown beef on all sides in a skillet with hot fat or oil. This gives a beautiful color that stays with the meal all the way. Place beef in a steamer rack, cover, and steam for three hours. Then add carrots, potatoes and onions to second rack. Steam for thirty minutes. During final fifteen minutes, add cabbage and parsnips to third rack. Keep covered tightly throughout, but check the amount of liquid from time to time and add more water as needed.

Sauce for Pot au Feu

Strain out vegetables and herbs from steaming liquid and skim off excess fat. For a more concentrated flavor, reduce over high heat, and serve in a hot bowl. Dust finely chopped parsley over it.

Presentation Let the beef rest for ten minues and carve in slices. Serve on a big, heated platter with beef at one end. Fanning out from it, alternate cabbage wedges and carrot strips. On one side, stack turnips and onions; on the other, the potatoes. Chop more of the fresh herbs and sprinkle over the handsome dish. Garnish generously with watercress. Spoon a little sauce over the platter and pass the rest.

Serve with California Zinfandel, sourdough bread and sweet butter. Finish with steamed apples in brandy and cream.

Poule au pot

If on the night you plan to serve your pot au feu, the phone rings and you find yourself with some extra company, you can quickly acquire a whole chicken and toss it into the pot with everything else. It will take about an hour to cook, you'll stay unfrazzled and your guests will be dazzled.

Choucroute Garnie (Alsatian)

I had not even seen sauerkraut since I was a child, until, several years ago, French friends in San Francisco invited me to dinner and served choucroute garnie. This sounded a lot more respectable and interesting than sauerkraut, and indeed, was delicious and appealing. As with most of the meals-in-one-pot, it is heavier, heartier fare, better suited to cool weather, roaring fires and healthy appetites. In San Francisco, that can mean most of the year.

Germany and France are headquarters for choucroute garnie, but it is, above all, identified with Alsace, which of course has been both German and French.

Oddly enough, the best I have ever sampled was in Marseille, where, in need of a change after eating monumental amounts of seafood, I visited Le Chalet, a fine Alsatian restaurant several blocks from the center of town. The choucroute was memorable not only because it was delicious, but because they served me, solo that evening, enough food for a family of four.

Other diners at Le Chalet were in better training than I, for everyone seemed to have ordered quite serious first courses before they got down to the choucroute. At one table I observed plates of escargots, platters of cold sausages, terrines of pâté, baskets of vegetables and jugs of pickles. Of course, the other diners looked sturdy enough to handle all of this.

Choucroute garnie is another dish that varies from cook to cook and with the day's supply of good things at the market. Especially provocative is the flavor of gin that permeates the meat and sauerkraut, supplied by juniper berries or, if you choose, gin itself. (Don't tell me you don't like gin. You *will* like this.)

Meats may include any combination of the following: bacon, Polish sausages, smoked pork chops, Canadian style bacon, knockwurst, frankfurters, ham, pig's knuckles, pork loin spare ribs, braised duck or goose, and salt pork. Note that beef is not suggested with choucroute garnie.

We steam our choucroute in champagne or beer, and in about a half of the time many boiled or baked recipes suggest.

Choucroute Garnie

Serves eight

2 quarts champagne or beer
2 cups chicken stock or 6 chicken bouillon cubes
2 onions, chopped
3 large garlic cloves
1 teaspoon caraway seeds
2 bay leaves
20 juniper berries or ½ cup gin
2 pounds ham
2 Polish garlic sausages
2 pounds spareribs
6 frankfurters or knockwurst
½ pound salt pork
6 potatoes
Salt and pepper
4 pounds sauerkraut

Thoroughly wash and drain the sauerkraut in cold water, squeezing most of the water out with the fingers. A steamer rack serves as a colander.

Loosen the sauerkraut so the strands are free; avoid heavy, tightly-intertwined lumps.

Bring the champagne or beer, chicken stock, onions, garlic cloves, bay leaves, caraway seeds, and juniper berries to a boil, then reduce heat for a good, steamy simmer. On the first rack place the ham and potatoes, on the second rack the Polish sausages, knockwurst and spareribs; and on the third rack, the sauerkraut, mixed with thin slices of the salt pork. Steam one and one-quarter hours.

Strain vegetables and spices from steam liquid, skim off fat, reduce briefly over high heat, and serve as a delicious sauce.

Presentation Mound the sauerkraut in the center of a large, heated serving platter. Cut the ham into six wedges and arrange it, pointed side up, around the sauerkraut. Place the knockwurst or frankfurters vertically between the pieces of ham. Arrange one-quarter inch slices of Polish sausage around this base. Cut the spareribs apart and stack at one end of the platter on a bed of watercress; place potatoes at the other end on another bed of watercress. Pour some of the hot juices over the dish and dust with finely chopped parsley.

Serve with crusty French bread, dark rye and bagels. Have a good assortment of mustards, horseradish and little sour pickles, the best beer you can find, and a well chilled Gewurztraminer or a fine California Johannisburg Riesling.

Corned Beef and Cabbage (Irish)

Maybe it all began in Germany. Or the United States. Or China? Who knows? The important point is, most of us identify corned beef and cabbage with the Irish, and that is the way I intend to keep it compartmentalized.

It can be an absolutely delicious dish. And, then again, it can be a smelly, depressing concoction of watery corned beef and born-again, perhaps several times, cabbage. Few dishes can suffer the steam table blues more effectively.

All of which is entirely unnecessary, for corned beef and cabbage could hardly be easier to prepare. And the meat and vegetables complement each other beautifully.

Because of the extreme saltiness of fresh corned beef, it is a good idea to soak it for three or four hours in cold water, changing the water three or four times during that period. The so-called "mild-cured" corned beef now available needs no pre-soaking and cooks quickly, but lacks the great flavor we want.

It is wise to plan for leftovers, as well, for few meats are as good cold as this one. Cold "boiled" beef seems dull and uninteresting, while corned beef is terrific. A million delis can't be wrong.

Corned beef adapts well to steam cookery. In addition to cabbage, other vegetables that are tasty with it are broccoli, lima beans, green beans, leeks, turnips, celery, potatoes, and interestingly, baked beans.

Serves six

3½-4 pounds fresh corned beef, soaked to remove excess salt
1 large head cabbage, cut into six wedges
3 quarts water
3 stalks celery and leaves
2 carrots, chopped
2 onions, chopped
3 cloves garlic, chopped
12 peppercorns
6 whole cloves
2 bay leaves
1 lemon, chopped
Handful of parsley
6 chicken bouillon cubes
1 tablespoon fresh dill or ½ teaspoon dried dill
6 medium potatoes, peeled
6 slim carrots

To water add celery, chopped onions, carrots, garlic, lemon, peppercorns, herbs and spices, and bouillon cubes. Bring to a boil, then reduce heat enough to keep up a good head of steam, but *not* blow the lid off. Add corned beef to a steamer rack, cover, and steam for three hours. Once an hour check water level, and if too low, add another pint or so. After two and a quarter hours, add potatoes to second rack. Fifteen minutes later add carrots to the same rack. After fifteen more minutes add cabbage wedges to third rack. (Steam potatoes for forty-five minutes; carrots, thirty minutes; cabbage, fifteen minutes.)

Presentation Let meat stand about ten minutes after removing from steamer, letting it "set" which makes it easier to carve. Serve meat on a platter heavily garnished with watercress, with potatoes on each long side of the corned beef. Drizzle some of the steam liquid over meat and potatoes, then dust well with finely chopped fresh dill, or a mixture of dried dill and finely chopped fresh parsley.

Use a long oval or rectangular platter on which to alternate the cabbage wedges and handsome whole carrots. Drizzle melted butter over them, garnish with watercress, and again, dust with the dill or parsley.

Serve with mustard/mayonnaise sauce as well as good hot mustard and horseradish.

Paella (Spanish)

It's Spanish. It's delicious. It's famous in Kentucky and California and Maine. It's Paella. A wonderful combination of seafood, chicken and rice. At least.

The idea is similar to Couscous. But a different world of flavor and ingredients with an Iberian point of view. Not unrelated to many another catch-all, superb meal. But, the Spanish have a certain, unique, altogether entrancing manner in their cooking. I honestly don't know what it is. But, it works.

Serves six

1 2½-pound chicken, cut in pieces
12 prawns, shelled and deveined
12 clams
12 mussels
2 chorizos (or other gutsy, hot, garlicky sausages)
¼ cup olive oil
1 medium onion, chopped
2 cloves garlic, chopped
salt and pepper
2 cups rice
2½ cups chicken stock
1 cup clam juice
½ cup white wine
¼ teaspoon powdered saffron
¼ teaspoon ground coriander
½ teaspoon oregano
6 baby artichokes, trimmed and halved
1 large tomato, peeled, seeded and chopped
½ cup shelled, fresh peas
Pimentos and lemon wedges for garnish

Sauté chicken briefly in the bottom of the steampot in the olive oil with the onions, garlic, salt and pepper. Remove and place in one of the racks.

Add chicken stock, clam juice, wine, saffron, coriander and oregano to remaining oil, onions and garlic in bottom of steampot and stir, scraping. Place raw rice in a heat-proof bowl which will fit in one of the steamer racks with room to spare and pour liquid from bottom of steampot over it.

Next, add water and salt to bottom of steampot. Start steaming chicken for twenty minutes. Add sliced chorizo to chicken and at the same time insert the rice with the liquid into the middle level. Steam twenty minutes more.

Finally, in a third rack place the shellfish, artichokes and peas. Sprinkle the tomatoes on the rice. Keep rice on lowest level, shellfish and vegetables on next, and chicken and sausage on top. Make sure water is boiling well and there's plenty of steam. Then, turn off heat and leave for ten minutes without lifting lid.

It would be impossible to serve an unattractive paella. My suggestion is to find a platter large enough to accommodate everything. Toss the rice, chorizo and vegetables and place the chicken and shellfish upon it in an orderly way. Strips of pimentos and lemon wedges complete the picture.

Couscous (Moroccan)

Couscous is certainly the most famous dish from North Africa, where every country has its own version. Like pasta, its distant relative, it is made from semolina wheat, but its texture is much closer to that of a cereal grain.

In Morocco, couscous is prepared in a special pot called a couscoussière and our steamer makes a more-than-worthy substitute. Most of the couscous sold in America is of the instant-cooking variety, but we urge you not to follow the directions on the package, as you can so easily reproduce a more authentic and delectable dish by cooking it in the steamer.

Couscous appears on the menu not only as a main dish served with stewed meats, vegetables and spices, but, with the addition of honey, nuts and dried fruits, it makes a delicious dessert.

Frequently the term couscous refers to the entire meal-in-one-pot, and that is what we are concerned with here.

Serves eight

1 3½-4 pound chicken cut in pieces
2 pounds boneless lamb cut in cubes
¼ cup olive oil
4 carrots, sliced
2 onions cut in chunks
1½ quarts chicken stock
1 teaspoon cinnamon
1 teaspoon cloves
1 teaspoon cumin
½ teaspoon turmeric
pinch powdered saffron
Salt and pepper
2 cups couscous
4 zucchini, sliced
½ cup seedless raisins
1 can chick peas
3 tablespoons olive oil
pine nuts
fresh mint

Brown chicken and lamb briefly in the bottom of the steampot in the olive oil. Place in first rack with carrots and onions. Add chicken stock and spices to bottom of the steampot and steam for forty-five minutes.

Soak couscous in cold water for five minutes. Line one of the steamer racks with cheesecloth and when the meat and vegetables have finished their forty-five minutes, insert couscous rack so that it cooks at the middle level. At the same time, add zucchini, raisins and chick peas to the meat and vegetables. If you find yourself running out of space, add a third rack.

After the couscous has steamed for fifteen minutes, remove, sprinkle with olive oil and mix with fingers so that each grain is coated. Steam everything for ten more minutes.

Serve the meats and vegetables on a bed of couscous, pour on a generous quantity of the fragrant steam liquid and garnish with pine nuts and fresh mint.

Chicken Babylon

My friend Idalene Allman is a busy executive who also manages to be a good interior designer, marvelous gardener and spectacular cook. We bachelors know how to get to this sort of person, and present our most forlorn, TV dinner-junk food personalities to them.

Naturally, the Idalenes of this world are distressed enough to come rushing around with breads, cakes, cookies, relishes, pepper jelly, pots of this and that. When you visit their homes, they prepare specialties you would never cook for yourself.

Idalene's Chicken Jerusalem is one of those, which she has revised for the steampot, and now calls

Chicken Babylon

Serves six

1 4-pound roasting chicken
1 pound thinly sliced fresh
   mushrooms
6 artichoke bottoms
1 large shallot, chopped
Flour
2 tablespoons butter
1 cup cream
Salt and pepper
pinch nutmeg
½ cup Sherry
Chopped parsley

Flour chicken lightly, and then brown in a heavy skillet in butter. Remove chicken, then add shallots and sauté until just soft. Add salt, pepper, nutmeg and sherry and cook a few minutes over moderate heat. Place chicken in an ovenproof bowl or platter that will fit into the steamer. Pour shallot mixture over chicken, and steam for twenty-five minutes. Add mushrooms and artichokes. Steam for five more minutes. Remove from heat, add the cream, another sprinkling of sherry, and fresh, finely chopped parsley. Coat chicken well with the liquid, and pop under broiler for a couple of minutes to brown. Serve bubbling and piping hot.

Steamed Chicken, Herbs and Vegetables

Serves six

1 4-pound roasting chicken
1 tablespoon salt for steaming
    liquid
1 medium onion
2 medium carrots
Handful of fresh parsley, bay
    leaves, oregano and thyme
½ lemon
olive oil
Salt and freshly ground pepper

Slice carrots, chop onions and lemon. Mix with herbs and about one teaspoon salt. Stuff chicken and pin or sew cavity together. Brush with olive oil and grind a lot of pepper on the chicken. Place over high steam, for one hour.

Remove from steam and brown in a hot oven for five minutes. (This is not necessary, unless you insist chicken should be brown or golden. As it comes from the steamer, it is a handsome yellow color. Just dust it heavily with finely chopped parsley or more of the same herbs you used for stuffing.)

Open the chicken and the aromatic steam rushes forth. The vegetables, heavily herbed, are delicious. Of course, there are not enough in the cavity to serve six. Twenty-five minutes before the chicken is finished, place halved, unpeeled potatoes in a rack and steam at the lowest level and in fifteen minutes add another rack with more carrots and onions. The chicken, because of its dimension, should be on the rack directly under the domed lid.

Remember, although there are many types of effective steamers, throughout this book we use the steampot, an aluminum variation of the classic oriental bamboo rack steamers. The prime difference is that this metal steamer has its own pot whereas the oriental ones are normally used over woks.

Keep in mind that all of my steam schemes began with a large strainer or colander over a pot of boiling water. But the steampot, with its tightly fitting domed lid, is faster, more efficient, and does a better job of recirculating those remarkable steam juices. The high, domed lid is necessary when you steam chicken, turkey, any meat over three inches high, or when you are using a bowl that may be higher than the rack.

Back to the menu: tender, moist chicken, vegetables and potatoes, all well flavored with onions and herbs. Add to this crusty sourdough bread, sweet butter, good robust wine, possibly an apple or pear with a wedge of honest cheese for dessert. There is a forthright, no-nonsense, down-on-the-farm quality about this meal that is uncomplex and appealing.

If you'll be reasonably prudent about the sourdough bread and butter, and exercise modest control about the amount of everything you eat and drink at this meal, I think you'll find it to be a rousing success in your skinny, beautiful campaign. It's nutritious, delicious and quite simple to prepare.

Variations Other vegetables that work well in the stuffing include leeks, celery, small artichokes, young parsnips and green beans. Garlic adds an interesting flavor, as does a dried bay leaf. Experiment. Come up with your own solutions!

Top: Robert C. Gray, Jr. Spaulding Taylor, Sallie Kelly, Flor Georges-Picot, Charlotte Mailliard, Jack Mailliard, Kayla Grodsky, John Bricker, Ruth Miller, Gerold Grodsky
Bottom: Joseph Andrews, Dennis Hearne, Monica Thigh, Maur Miller, Monique Bertrand, Matthew Kelly, Lita Vietor, Eugene Kenney, C. Camilleri, Jean McClatchy

SEAFOOD STEAM TRIPS
IN SAN FRANCISCO

San Franciscans are often accused of being smug, overbearing and boring as we rhapsodize about the wondrous mysteries and blessings of this fabled city.

From its rare beauty, its remarkable mixture of people, its intriguing ethnic quarters, its crisp, sparkling weather (counterpointed with our private air conditioner, the fog), its amazing number of fine restaurants—to the abundance of outstanding markets where the most tempting foods are always available, San Francisco is special. So we'll continue to indulge ourselves, to wallow in chauvinistic pride that we are so fortunate to live here.

All of which leads to the fact that among our blessings is the availability of the freshest, most delectable seafood. This includes our rightly-famous Dungeness crab, mouthwatering rex sole and petrale, sand dabs, tiny shrimp and large prawns, our fabulous salmon, squid, scallops, clams, oysters, sea bass, Pacific lobster, crayfish, trout, striped bass, flounder and eel. And of course the incomparable abalone.

It seems unfair to add that San Franciscans have been given even more wonderful things for their tables. Crusty, sourdough bread. Beautiful fresh fruits and vegetables. Wines that rival the greatest in Europe, some with such limited production that they seldom move beyond San Francisco. Highly respectable local brie and camembert cheeses. Choice delicacies from our international sections: Chinese, Japanese, Italian, Russian, Middle Eastern, Mexican, Philippino, and South Sea Island.

Seafood takes to steam like peaches to cream. It is a perfect method of cooking to preserve the fleeting, subtle flavors of

19

shrimp and clams, of keeping sea bass and salmon moist and tender, of tantalizing taste buds with the sinfully good Dungeness crab.

The moist, swirling heat of steam really is a superior method of cooking most seafood. I cannot conceive an instance when boiling would be better, nor is baking, with the exception of last minute toasting or browning, as good. (I do not, I hasten to affirm, advise giving up a beautiful piece of rex sole or petrale, gently sauteed in butter, which is even better than the celebrated Dover sole. In *my* opinion.)

Here, we'll suggest some effective recipes for both fish and crustaceans, meals-in-one-pot, and a few ideal menus.

Mary Ri's Steamed San Francisco Seafood Soiree

Mary Ri, a talented interior designer, is equally noted for her artistry in the kitchen. Flair and creativity are part of her work, her home, her look, her cooking and entertainment.

Recently, she decided to create a monumental seafood dinner in one pot. The steampot. What else? The occasion was an informal Sunday evening in San Francisco. There were four of us, an ideal number for experimental cooking, as well as relaxed conversation.

Wonderful beach dinners on the New England coast were her inspiration. There, big metal drums were half-filled with water, seaweed and rock salt, and then, on improvised racks, stacks of clams and prawns, slabs of cod fish, potatoes in their skins and corn on the cob were all steamed together. Mary figured it could be scaled down and converted to the kitchen.

Our first order of business was to go shopping. Because we needed seaweed, we decided to go to San Francisco's Japan Town. At an excellent market we found gleaming fresh fish and prawns, and tightly closed clams on beds of greenery. Here too we got a package of dried seaweed, good soy sauce, and Japanese sesame cookies.

We went to another market and bought potatoes, young ears of sweet corn, artichokes right off the truck from Castroville, "artichoke capital of the world," and deep red, spring strawberries. We picked up French baguettes and a slab of freshly churned sweet butter on Union Street. The lemons and parsley we picked from my deck.

For the first course, Mary steamed tender, trimmed artichokes with a lemony mayonnaise dressing. Next, the meal-in-one-pot, a humble name for a culinary triumph of considerable proportions.

In a vast, flat wooden bowl, she placed a beautifully steamed, thick section of sea bass, surrounded by steaming clams, interspersed with mounds of those pink prawns with the ultra thin shells that can be eaten. Tiny new potatoes and four-inch sections of corn of the cob, garnished with bundles of parsley and lemon wedges completed this superb still life.

With it she served small cups of the delicious steam broth, each with a thin slice of lemon floating on top. There was another pitcher of sauce on the table.

The wine was 1976 Cairanne, Côtes du Rhone. This is an unusually strong, crisp, dry white wine and a perfect choice for the meal. Tom Jurgensen, manager of the main Jurgensen's store in San Francisco, tells me this is the most popular French white their stores sell.

For a light dessert to complement the hearty meal, Mary served fresh strawberries, laced with Cointreau and brown sugar and a dollop of crème fraiche on each serving. The strawberries were garnished with sprigs of mint. A

Japanese sesame seed cookie added the final note. Gutsy French roast coffee topped everything to perfection.

Steamed San Francisco Seafood Soiree

Serves four

1 pound uncooked prawns in the shell
1 pound sea bass or cod
2 dozen clams
1 large leaf dried seaweed
Bunch of parsley
½ cup sea salt or rock salt
2 tablespoons soy sauce
2 medium onions, chopped
3 lemons
16 small new potatoes, unpeeled
4 ears of corn

First, simmer the seaweed with a little water in a saucepan for fifteen minutes. Then add it, the salt, soy sauce, chopped onions, handful of parsley and more water to the steampot. Squeeze the juice of a lemon into the pot, then coarsely chop the rind and toss it in as well. Bring to full steam.

On first rack, place potatoes, and on the second rack, the sea bass, assuming it is a thick piece as we had. Steam for eight minutes. Then add corn, broken into half ears, to the fish rack. On the third rack place clams and prawns. Steam everything for five to seven more minutes. (If any clams remain closed, steam them for three more minutes; if still closed, discard.)

One of Mary Ri's tricks is to pierce the potatoes at three or four points with a sharp knife, permitting faster cooking, but also helping the wonderful steamy juices to penetrate the potatoes.

Presentation Place fish in center of a large, flat wooden bowl or platter. Ring the prawns around the fish. Next, alternate mounds of clams and potatoes. Put the ears of corn around the outer part of the bowl. Garnish generously with clusters of parsley and lemon wedges. Spoon more of the steam stock over the entire combination, and dust it with finely chopped parsley. Grind lots of fresh pepper over it, too. Provide each guest with an oriental bowl or small cup of the liquid and float a thin slice of lemon on top.

Steamed Seafood Stew

Serves six

3½ pounds sea bass, cod or other firm, white-fleshed fish
1 bottle Chablis or other dry white wine
24 small white onions
2 cups chopped carrots
½ cup lemon juice
4 garlic cloves
2 bay leaves
Handful fresh parsley, thyme and dill
1½ pounds mushrooms
6 large slices French bread, one-inch thick

Pour wine into steampot and add onions, carrots and lemon juice. Chop the garlic and put it in a cheesecloth bag with bay leaf and most of the fresh herbs. (Reserve the remainder of the herbs for garnish.) Bring to high steam.

Meanwhile, slice French bread on the diagonal for large slices, brush both sides with butter, and toast until golden.

Place fish on first steamer rack. Quarter the mushrooms and add to the second. Steam together for eight minutes. Remove from heat. Discard bay leaves and garlic from steam liquid, reduce over high heat to half its volume and serve as sauce.

Place warm toasted French bread in heated soup bowls. At table, serve a portion of fish on each, with mushrooms, onions and carrots. Ladle on some of the steam stock and dust with more of the chopped herbs.

Follow this with a light salad, then fruit and hearty cheese for dessert. Serve with a good Pinot Chardonnay or California Reisling.

Steamed Oysters
à la Provençale

Serves four

24 oysters
½ cup good olive oil
1 medium onion, well chopped
4 medium tomatoes
1 tablespoon finely chopped garlic
Salt and pepper
2 tablespoons finely chopped
    parsley and oregano
¼ cup dried breadcrumbs
3 cups white wine
2 lemons

In a skillet, sauté the onion, to-matoes, garlic, salt, pepper, parsley and oregano in olive oil for about six minutes. Stir in bread crumbs. Remove from heat.

To steampot, add wine, juice of one lemon, one teaspoon salt and ground pepper. Bring to high steam and add oysters to first rack. Steam for six to seven min-utes, or a bit longer if they have not opened. Add steam liquid to tomato sauce, reduce until thick, and spoon over oysters. Serve on a platter with lemon wedges.

Start this meal with cold leeks or asparagus vinaigrette. With the oysters serve crusty French bread and sweet butter. Dessert might be a steamed pear or apple, or perhaps a wedge of fresh hon-eydew melon. A perfect meal for staying skinny, beautiful and suc-cessful.

Steamed Curried Clams

Serves four

32 small clams
¼ cup olive or peanut oil
1 tablespoon finely chopped
    ginger root
3 medium onions
1 teaspoon salt
1½ teaspoons dried coriander
1 teaspoon turmeric
¼ cup shredded coconut
1 tablespoon chopped cilantro
    (Chinese parsley)
½ teaspoon hot red pepper
    ground
1 tablespoon lemon juice

In the bottom of the steampot, heat the oil and stir in the ginger. Add onions, which should be thinly sliced. Stir fry over moderate heat for six to seven minutes, or until they are golden brown. Add salt, coriander and turmeric, stir and cook a minute or so more, then add clams. Care-fully toss clams in the mixture to make certain they are well coated with the curry. Cover pot and steam clams for ten minutes, and a minute or so more if any have not opened. Discard any that won't open within a few more minutes. Serve on a heated plat-ter, carefully scraping the pan for every delicious bit. Dust with chopped cilantro (or parsley), coconut, red pepper, and sprinkle with lemon juice. Serve, with the smug knowledge you've done it. Again.

Steamed
Dungeness Crab

It's almost a redundancy to speak of cracked crab, sourdough French bread and a chilled bottle of white wine in the same breath as San Francisco. That menu can *only* mean San Francisco. It just isn't the same anywhere else.

That wonderful Pacific Dunge-ness Crab is never as sweet, never as tender, never as seductive as it is here. The bread? Nowhere this side of Paris is the bread better, and in my experience, not always there either.

It is always amusing to see our great bread being shipped off to Los Angeles or Dallas or Chicago.

Or to watch the tourists buying it by the ton at the airport.

The sad truth is, the bread must be baked and eaten *here*. Preferably today. (Actually, it can be resurrected to a reasonable degree, when it is a day or so old, by wrapping it in foil and heating it in the oven. The serious, but altogether understandable problem is that most of the bakeries that create this culinary masterpiece do not work Tuesday nights, which means no fresh bread on Wednesdays.)

Fortunately, all is not lost. There are a few, noble small bakeries in our North Beach area that do bake *every* day. Bless them. They even bake on Christmas morning. Cuneo and Danilo are two that spring to mind.

But, man cannot live by bread alone, as has been written. He must have further communion with the good earth, indeed, with the vine. A scant forty miles from San Francisco begin the lovely meadows and hillsides of the Napa Valley with its celebrated vineyards. Close by are Sonoma, its important neighbor, Mendocino County to the northwest, Lake County to the east.

Great cooking in the Bay Area dates from the days of the Gold Rush, when the great chefs of Europe flocked to San Francisco to cater to all the big spenders and high livers. They soon became aware of the similarities of Northern California to those regions of Europe where the great wines were born. The word spread. Soon more Europeans came, bringing with them their precious cuttings of the finest vines of France, Italy, Germany, Hungary and Austria.

From these beginnings, through ups and downs, including the dark days of Prohibition, California wines gradually came into their own, and many of them, today, rival the world's finest. We are becoming accustomed to blind tastings where famous French vintners select a California wine over their own. Mortifying as it is, some of the great Frenchmen have revised their estimates of the possibilities of California wines. Vast volumes of wine are produced in California. And those which win the prizes are all within close orbit of San Francisco.

Further, again in my opinion, our bulk wines are normally better than French vin ordinaire. Perhaps I mean the average "house wine" you find in Paris. From time to time you'll discover a restaurant with its own special source of top-notch table wine. Occasionally in the provinces you'll find a fabulous vin ordinaire. (This has often happened to me in Italy.) But, by and large, our own bulk wines are without peer in this category.

Great Scott!! I'm getting steamed up about California wine and San Francisco sourdough bread when we're trying to discuss crab. But afficionados of crab will *know* the importance of what I have said. Because crab, while delicious at breakfast, brunch, lunch, dinner, cocktails, late night snack and in-between, requires good bread and good wine.

Purist Steamed Crab

Many a crab lover will not tolerate variations or embellishments of pure, simple, superb, undisguised crabmeat, hot or cold. Happily, preparation is simplicity itself. Just buy cooked crab at the market, place over high steam for three minutes—or just long enough to heat, and serve with a boat of melted butter and lemon juice. Purists prefer to dig the crabmeat out of the shells themselves.

If you buy live crabs (I don't like to cope with anything moving around the kitchen under its own steam, so to speak), steam them until they turn bright orange. This will take from twelve to fifteen minutes.

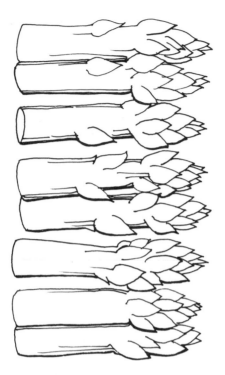

Steamed Crab and Asparagus au Gratin

Serves four

2 pounds cooked crab meat
1 tablespoon salt for steaming liquid
2 pounds asparagus
¼ cup freshly grated Parmesan cheese
¼ cup freshly grated Swiss cheese
½ cup heavy cream
Freshly ground black pepper
2 teaspoons chopped chives

Snap off ends of asparagus, peel and steam for eight minutes over salted water. In second rack heat crab for about two minutes. On an ovenproof serving platter, arrange asparagus, and on top of that, the crabmeat. Sprinkle with one and then the other grated cheese and cover with heavy cream. Grind pepper over everything and dust with chopped chives. Place in a hot oven (500°) for five minutes, or until the topping is bubbly and golden.

Garnish with sprigs of watercress. Serve for brunch with sliced tomatoes, quartered artichoke hearts and a good, dry white wine.

Crab With Artichoke Hearts

Serves four

2 pounds cooked crab meat
16 small Italian artichokes
1 tablespoon salt for steam liquid
4 tablespoons butter
3 tablespoons chopped shallots
2 tablespoons chopped fresh tarragon (¼ teaspoon dried. It's quite strong.)
½ cup dried bread crumbs

Ruthlessly strip away outer tough leaves from the artichokes and trim top and bottom. Steam for ten minutes in first rack over salted water. Add crab meat in second rack for a couple of minutes, simply to heat. Sauté shallots and tarragon in butter over a low heat for five minutes. Stir in bread crumbs for a few more minutes. Combine with crab and artichokes, garnish with more fresh tarragon or watercress, and serve.

Steamed Crab, Prawns and Clams

Serves four

2 medium crabs, cracked
8 large prawns
16 clams
2 onions
2 carrots
2 stalks celery
4 cloves garlic, chopped
½ cup vinegar
½ cup olive oil
1 tablespoon salt
12 peppercorns
Handful of fresh herbs

Make a court bouillon for the steaming liquid with roughly chopped carrots, celery, onions, garlic, oil, vinegar, salt, peppercorns and herbs. Steam clams and prawns from five to eight minutes on first rack, discarding any clams that do not open. On second rack, heat the crab for three minutes.

Make a colorful mixture of the seafood on a large platter garnished with sprigs of watercress. An ideal starter would be a good pasta al pesto. After the seafood, offer a green salad, loaves of crusty Italian bread, and white wine served in husky glass liters.

Steamed Salmon Steaks in Dill

Serves four

4 thick salmon steaks
1 tablespoon salt for steam liquid
10 peppercorns
Handful of fresh dill

Add salt, peppercorns and handful of dill to steam liquid. Steam salmon steaks on first rack for seven minutes. Serve at once with pat of lemon-dill butter on top.

Lemon-dill Butter

½ cup sweet butter
2 tablespoons lemon juice
2 tablespoons chopped fresh dill

The lemon-dill butter should be prepared beforehand as follows: Soften the butter, add chopped fresh dill and lemon juice a drop at a time. Cream together, form into a short roll about one and one-half inches in diameter. Roll in wax paper and refrigerate to firm. Then, cut into slices to garnish salmon.

This dish is good with crisply steamed snow peas, tiny new potatoes in their jackets and a fine California Pinot Chardonnay or a

French Pouilly Fuissé. The perfect meal for skinny, beautiful people. Low in calories, high in nutrition and absolutely delicious.

Variation Place under broiler for one minute, then serve at once. The hot dill butter melting over the fish is aromatic and appetizing.

Chilled Steamed Salmon

Serves six

4-5 pound center cut fresh
  salmon
2 onions
2 medium carrots
3 stalks celery
Handful of fresh herbs
½ cup vinegar
½ cup olive oil
Chopped chives
1 tablespoon salt
12 peppercorns
1 lemon

Add all the ingredients except the salmon to three quarts of water. Onions, carrots, celery and herbs should be chopped. The lemon should be squeezed and chopped and both juice and rind included in the stock. Bring to high steam.

Wrap a cheesecloth sling around the salmon and steam-poach it on the first rack for forty minutes. Remove from heat. Strain steam

liquid and discard vegetables. Carefully place salmon still in the cheesecloth, into liquid and let cool.

Spread a thin coating of mustard mayonnaise over the salmon (by now, you will have discarded the cheesecloth), dust with chopped chives and serve, with additional mustard mayonnaise at the table. This could be accompanied by chilled leeks vinaigrette and cherry tomatoes, crusty French baguettes and a chilled bottle of California Pinot Chardonnay. Fantastic!

VAPORS VEGETABLES AND VICTORIES

Vegetables have had a bum rap for a long time. Most of us started out hating them as children, gradually tolerated some, and eventually found that they can be pretty good.

Unfortunately, vegetables are often abused in the kitchen. Most of them are crisp and delicious raw, but become dull, tasteless and boring after they are man-handled in restaurants or rendered unappetizing by insensitive home cooks.

The main problem is that most vegetables are overcooked most of the time. Granted, some of us prefer ours less cooked than others, but: green beans were not intended to be cooked until they become dark gray. Carrots were not created to be boiled limp and lifeless. Potatoes were never meant to be mushy. Cabbage is not supposed to become a soggy, smelly mess, the odors of which invade the entire house. Asparagus was not intended to be cooked to the consistency of wet toast. Peas were certainly not destined to become mushy, gray pellets that turn to puree when touched with a fork.

No. Vegetables are beautiful. Small wonder they are often featured in still life paintings, or used for outstanding table centerpieces. At their best they are crisp, fresh and handsomely green, yellow, white, red, purple, or orange (never gray).

Contrary to what we have seen most of our lives—in fact, practically every day—vegetables when cooked should retain that marvelous freshness, that crisp texture, that same appeal that they had when raw. They should be adequately cooked, yet al dente, the fine Italian expression that means soft, yet resistant to the bite. Normally this phrase is used when referring to pasta, but I like it for vegetables, too.

The Italians and French do understand vegetables and know how to select and cook them to retain their wondrous garden-fresh look and taste. The French often blanch their vegetables, which means they partially cook them in boiling water, "refresh" them under cold water, and, just before serving, reheat them quickly with butter or a sauce.

We'll do exactly that, with the refinement that our vegetables will be steamed, and will not have lost any flavor or nutrients in water that will be thrown away. Oriental cuisine features beautifully undercooked, delicious vegetables. But that subject is not for this book. (See *The Great Asia Steambook* by Irene Wong for the exciting possibilities of oriental steam cooking.) Other nations, which shall remain nameless, often, I fear, miss the entire point of cooking fresh, appealing vegetables. Instead the vegetables tend to stew on a back burner for hour after dreary hour.

Overcooking vegetables is a *sin*. Don't be guilty.

I seldom peel any vegetable. Scrape, scrub, shake, rub, wash, brush, wipe, soak or any other method you may devise for cleaning a specific vegetable. But why peel away half the food value, and perhaps the tastiest part of the potato, the eggplant or the cucumber?

You can, of course, scrape vegetables with any knife, but I find the kind with a serrated edge the easiest to use. A tough, plastic-fiber pot walloper can be effec-

tive, as can the small, sand paper-like pieces of cloth that are also used for cleaning pots. Best of all, I've found, is a small metal brush that is sold as a stove cleaning brush. It's easy to use and highly effective when cleaning carrots, potatoes, parsnips, celery, beets and other root vegetables.

The only time to peel potatoes, in my opinion, is when they are to be mashed or whipped, which I never do in any event. I do peel the lower part of the asparagus, although this should not be necessary if you can find sensitive, young, tender spears. For this, there is a fine gadget with a flexible, floating blade that easily strips away the outer skin.

To me, the appearance of food is as important as the taste. Vegetables can be presented with great flair and style, but without a belabored, contrived appearance. Vegetables should be served whole, when reasonable, or cut into interesting shapes that have a logical relationship to their structure and are easy to eat. As an example, let us take carrots, which I find far more appealing to eat when cut into julienne strips rather than in hunks or slices. If not too large, they are handsome whole, especially if they are young and gracefully slim. Better still are small French-type carrots now appearing in our California

markets; perhaps in yours, too. Whole carrots will take somewhat longer to steam, depending on size.

Typical round slices of carrots do not interest me unless they are used as a design counterpoint to long vegetables or vegetables cut in strips, such as green beans, asparagus, mild chilis, bell peppers, celery or leeks. Carrots are nice if sliced on the diagonal as the Orientals do. This way of preparation can be effective, too, with zucchini, cucumbers, broccoli stalks, radishes, celery and even large green beans.

Avoid hunks and chunks. Rather, plan to serve strips, wedges, stalks, slivers, slices and curls. (Steamed carrot curls are attractive and delicious, and you will certainly be first on your block to serve them.) I'm anti diced vegetables. Of course, they do have their place from time to time, but they remind me of dreary canned vegetables or those insipid canned soups. Sorry, no dice.

Full Steam. Ahead.

We mentioned blanching vegetables in the French, boiling water method. Far better, steam-blanch them. Just steam the vegetables a few minutes less than the recipe suggests, refresh under cold water to stop the cooking. Just before you are ready to serve the meal, toss them in a skillet at high heat with butter, lemon juice and fresh cracked pepper, and arrange on a hot platter or individual dinner plates.

This steam-blanch method has several advantages. You finish some of the work before the guests arrive. The cooking odors—seldom as intriguing with vegetables as with meats, fruits or baked goods—are gone when the party begins. You have more time for other details at that critical moment when the meal is coming together. You see more of your guests. And, if you have a small apartment as I do, the living room does not look like a steam bath as the guests are trying to find their martinis on the cocktail table.

Vegetable Steamtips

•When you steam two, three or four vegetables at the same time, place those that must cook the longest in the bottom steamer level. You can add more levels at later times for those that require less cooking. For example, you may have whole potatoes on the bottom. They'll cook for thirty minutes. After eight minutes, add green beans on the second level. They'll cook for seventeen minutes. Finally, add tiny white "boiling" onions to the third level for the last ten minutes. All are superbly cooked at the same moment.

• Always turn on your kitchen exhaust fan while steaming. If you don't have one, open a couple of windows for cross draft. Otherwise you'll steam up everything in sight.

I have never found a vegetable that does not taste delicious steamed.

• Under, rather than over cook.

Openers and Hors d'oeuvres

For hors d'oeuvres and meal openers when you don't plan to serve salad, offer baskets of steam-blanched vegetables. They look great, taste great, and marvelously complement a good stiff Jack Daniels, a Margarita, a Martini, a glass of wine or *any* spirits.

The vegetables are neither raw nor cooked. They've been quickly, gently steamed just enough to make them a bit more interesting to the bite from a textural point of view, and just enough to have triggered some taste explosions that are highly satisfying.

Some good choices would be: zucchini, peppers, carrots, parsnips, leeks, summer squash, cucumbers cut into long strips, large mushrooms cut in half, whole green beans (stringed), asparagus (peeled), whole small artichokes (with *all* the tough outer petals stripped away), trimmed celery stalks, small onions, broccoli flowerets and whole snow peas. If you can float a loan, splurge on Belgium endive. If not, ruthlessly strip off the outer leaves of romaine until you're down to that crisp, tempting heart. (Save the other leaves for something else.)

Preparation Heat a couple of quarts of water until it is furiously boiling, add vegetables to various racks (lettuce on top), steam one minute, and then refresh everything under cold water, and perhaps even cover with ice water. As you'll recall, the idea is to stop any further cooking and softening of the crisp vegetables.

Presentation Serve on platters with a tangy sauce in the center, or in handsome baskets, with various sauces available for dipping. Here is another great opportunity to do a culinary painting or fine sculpture.

I find these steam-blanched vegetables the perfect prelude to grilled steaks with green peppercorn butter and sizzling potato puffs followed by tart pears and Brie, the cheese preferred by steamers the world over.

The Cold Vegetable Spectacular

Do this one well and you'll have it made as an outstanding cook, host or hostess. It really is spectacular. It really is delicious. And, there is no limit to how creative you can be with this beautiful culinary construction. Further, it is so simple that all you need is your steampot, a large platter, any number of super fresh vegetables and a minimum of time.

Presentation Serve on a large, round platter, preferably about fifteen inches in diameter. Place cauliflower in the center, with spokes of red or green bell pepper on top. Surround with snow peas in neat order. Next, arrange a ring of sliced zucchini, carefully overlapped. Finally, at six outer points, fan out clusters of watercress. The taste is great.

With it, serve a hot or cold roast, a steamed or roasted chicken, a steamed salmon, or a cold tongue in aspic. Offer your guests three sauces: a simple, but delectable vinaigrette; the superb warm anchovy sauce, Italian bagno caudo, and our own simple sour cream mustard sauce.

Remember, in creating the vegetable spectacular, almost any fresh vegetable can be used. Think of the design possibilities with artichoke hearts, asparagus, celery, radishes, mushrooms, tomatoes, Frenched green beans, tiny new potatoes, leeks or broccoli. Not only are you dealing with good taste combinations, you have at your creative disposal all the colors, shapes, and textures of the garden.

1 medium cauliflower
6 medium zucchini
1 pound snow peas
2 bell peppers (red or green or
    both)
1 large bunch watercress
3 quarts basic steam liquid

Cauliflower—Remove all outer leaves. Cut off bottom stem. Wash. Steam in lowest rack for ten minutes. Refresh under cold water.

Zucchini—Wash. Do not peel. Slice on diagonal. Steam on second rack for four minutes. Refresh under cold water.

Snow peas—Snap off ends and remove strings from both sides. Wash. Don't shell. Steam on top rack for four minutes. Refresh under cold water.

Bell peppers—Wash. Cut off stem and core. Seed. Cut into vertical strips one-quarter inch in width. Steam on top rack with snow peas for four minutes.

The Steaming Vegetable Centerpiece

This is one of the inumerable variations on the cold spectacular, but served piping hot. Substitute any vegetables you like and that are congenial together. Here, we'll use broccoli, new potatoes in their skins, small, whole onions and cherry tomatoes.

The vegetables should be timed to finish steaming at the same moment. The potatoes start first in the lowest rack; next the onions go into the second rack, then the broccoli, and finally, the tomatoes go into the top rack briefly, yet not so long that they turn mushy and lose their shape.
Serves six

18 medium or 24 small new
    potatoes
1 pound white boiling onions
2 pounds broccoli
2 dozen cherry tomatoes
one large lemon for garnish

Potatoes—Scrub with wire brush or pot walloper. Do not peel or cut. Steam on first rack for thirty-five minutes. (Fewer potatoes take less time.) Check with fork to test. You may like them cooked a bit softer.

Onions—Peel and trim ends and place on second rack. If the onions are small (one to one and one-half inches in diameter), they'll steam in ten minutes. If larger, plan on extra minutes.

Broccoli—Trim off all but about two or three inches of stem. (Remainder can be steamed another day as a vegetable or soup.) Arrange in second rack with the onions, stems towards the center. Steam eight minutes. Fork test.

Cherry Tomatoes—Wash, trim stems. Steam in top rack for three minutes. Do not allow them to

become too soft or sagging. It is best to take them from the steamer just before they split.

Overall cooking time is thirty-five minutes. So, to save you all the mathematics, the onions go on after the potatoes have been cooking twenty-five minutes. In two minutes add the broccoli, and then the tomatoes after another five. Three minutes more of steaming and it's all done.

Lemon Mustard Butter Sauce

½ cup sweet butter
Juice of 1 lemon
2 tablespoons Dijon mustard
Salt and pepper
Finely chopped parsley or chives

Melt the butter in pan, add lemon juice, mustard, salt to taste and generous grindings of good black pepper. Toss in a handful of finely chopped parsley or chives.

Presentation Mound potatoes in center of platter. Fan out six clusters of broccoli at equal intervals around them. Place several tomatoes between the stalks of broccoli and arrange the onion at their outer edge. By each portion of broccoli, place a wedge of lemon. Just before serving, ladle hot lemon mustard butter sauce over this brilliant conversation piece-centerpiece.

Artichokes

They came from France and Italy. But I identify them with California's foggy, coastal area between San Francisco and Monterey. Artichokes. A beautiful flower if left to ripen. But, more importantly to this discussion, a wondrous, tightly-petaled, unopened bud; an elegant member of the thistle family.

They are a natural for an impressionist still life. A photographer's dream. Basic to *Gourmet* covers. An essential to the cuisines of Julia and Jim and M.F.K. and Michael. And, happily, they require minimal effort in preparation.

The simple life: a loaf of bread, a jug of wine and thou. Especially if thou wouldst bring along a steamed artichoke. Perhaps a bowl of your own homemade mayonnaise, alerted with a nuance of hot mustard and an extra squeeze of lemon. Ah, to gaze into your eyes while stripping an artichoke through my teeth, then flipping the remains over my shoulder with carefree, yet studied, abandon. The good life.

Artichokes are one of my six favorite vegetables. They're intriguing. (Fatiguing, too, by the time you've shredded all those leaves with your teeth, scooped out the choke and carefully knifed and forked the bottom.)

They appear in numerous guises. Bottoms filled with shrimp and hollandaise. Hearts pristinely coated with lemon and butter to adorn a rack of lamb. Pickled. Dipped into mayonnaise and caviar. Filled with tiny peas. Stuffed full of flaked crabmeat.

Life is definitely a richer, more fulfulling experience thanks to the artichoke. Yet, caviar and crabmeat aside, all artichokes really require is correct steaming, and a little melted butter or mayonnaise.

Steamed Artichokes

The artichoke Select the freshest, greenest, most tightly closed artichokes you can find. Strip off the small outer leaves around the base. Cut off the stems even with the base so they will stand up in the pot and on the plate. With a sharp knife cut off the top sharply pointed tips. Trim each leaf with a scissors or sharp knife. Have half a lemon handy and rub all cut edges and surfaces at once to prevent discoloration. (You can place them in a bowl of cold water with half a cup of vinegar, too.)

The steam liquid To three quarts of water add ½ cup olive oil, several crushed garlic cloves, 1 tablespoon peppercorns, ¼ cup vinegar, ¼ cup lemon juice, 1 lemon, sliced, 2 tablespoons salt. Place artichokes in rack over high steam, covered of course, for forty-five minutes. Test in about forty minutes. Tear off a leaf and taste it. You'll know if it needs more steam time.

The sauce Serve hot artichokes with small pots or cups of melted butter and lemon juice and cold ones with homemade mayonnaise heavily accented with a good mustard. Or, add a pinch of dry mustard to sour cream.

Social comments You'll be judged by the manner in which you eat artichokes, so be forewarned. Discretion is advised when shredding them through your teeth. To maintain dignity requires a certain amount of adroitness and finesse. Diversionary tactics are helpful, too. You might, for example, wonder out loud if your cigarette really did fall between the sofa cushions.

Further, what you do with the remains of the leaves is a clue as to whether you're loutish or orderly and refined. Just mounding them up in a sort of garbage pile simply doesn't do. Each leaf is designed to fit nicely into the next, starting with the larger ones.

Stack them in an orderly circle around the plate, even concentric circles if need be. If a large, common, central receptacle has been provided, you can arrange the leaves in stripes, crosses, or create an amusing fan shape. This is creative refuse, an interesting post-culinary art form.

Asparagus

Asparagus is one of the beautiful vegetables. Perhaps the most delicious. Certainly, the most elegant. Easily, one of the simplest to prepare.

In many areas, its presence on the market heralds an early sign of spring. In California, we know spring is here when the price of asparagus drops from a winter peak of something horrible like $3.89 per pound to an appealing 79c per pound. In high season in a good year, this may drop to 49c. On days when your horoscope is good and your biorhythm chart is on a high curve, asparagus may even plummet to 39c per pound.

Actually, I am not all that pleased that so many vegetables and fruits are available year round. When everything is in the market all the time I think we lose our sense of wonder at Nature's magic, our anticipation. Strawberries and asparagus in the spring. Then, peaches and raspberries. Grapes

in high summer. Crisp apples in the fall. Pumpkins and cranberries in time for the holidays.

Back to asparagus. Tender, young asparagus is best, with the leaves, or petals at the tip, tightly closed. Almost any vegetable that has petal-like clusters should be firm and tightly closed when you purchase it. As with a rose, a bud is younger and will last longer than an open flower. Other examples are artichokes, broccoli, cauliflower, scallions, leeks, and lettuce.

To prepare, snap off the tougher ends of the asparagus. They'll usually break at just about the right point of tenderness. Then, use your handy little, floating blade vegetable peeler and peel each stalk a few inches from the flower clear to the end. The blade on the peeler will strip the thinnest peel. Actually, you'll find peeling is an economy, since the whole asparagus stalk can then be eaten.

God probably meant for asparagus to be steamed. As with all vegetables, it should never be overcooked, and the steamer provides the safest method of maintaining that excellent al dente quality we prefer. If asparagus is to be the featured vegetable at a meal, allow half a pound per person when buying.

Steam eight to ten minutes, depending upon how thick it is, and how much is in the rack. One sure test of doneness is to prod the asparagus with a fork. If you are not serving it at once, be sure to refresh it under cold water, and then, just before serving, place in high steam for one minute, or toss with butter and lemon in a hot skillet.

If you are steam-blanching the asparagus to serve as an hors d'oeuvre on its own or as a crunchy first course with other vegetables, steam one minute, then refresh under cold water.

The best ways to serve asparagus, in my opinion, are with hot lemon butter, a simple vinaigrette, or a tangy mustard mayonnaise. All three are good with either hot or cold asparagus, with the exception of the lemon butter, which only enhances the hot vegetable. Freshly ground or cracked black pepper is always delicious with it too.

We won't say too much about asparagus topped with hollandaise sauce, however wonderful it is, for that would not contribute favorably to the skinny, beautiful image we've worked so hard to achieve.

Too bad. For a great brunch dish is composed of a toasted English muffin topped with smoked ham and asparagus tips, all liberally enveloped with creamy hollandaise sauce and crowned with slices of black truffles. Or—a skillet of steamed asparagus, covered with heavy cream, thoroughly sprinkled with freshly grated Parmesan cheese, and gratinéed to bubbly, golden perfection under the broiler.

Put it out of your mind. Remember, few dishes are as pure and tempting as simple asparagus with lemon and butter. Steamed, of course.

Beets

It beats me, but I don't know why there seems to be so little culinary research about beets. There are a good many references to borscht, but, with few exceptions, no serious discussions of this perfectly pleasant vegetable. Pleasant *if* it is handled with intelligent concern.

Beets are often boring. Yet, if gently steamed when they are young, tender and ready to please, they really have an interesting contribution to make. I think they are at their best when treated respectfully as in the following recipe, a favorite of my mother's, and I have yet to taste an improvement of it.

One further word before we proceed, if you're going to have beets,

they should be *red*. You must therefore steam them before they have been peeled, and you must not cut off very much of the tops or roots. If you follow this procedure, you will avoid any trace of gray in your beets.

Cold Steamed Beets Vinaigrette

Serves four

1 pound small, young beets
¼ pound sliced Bermuda onions
1 tablespoon salt for steaming liquid
¼ cup olive oil
¼ cup lemon juice
Freshly cracked pepper
Handful of fresh herbs

Combine water, salt, olive oil, lemon juice, cracked pepper and fresh herbs in the bottom of the steamer. Steam unpeeled beets for thirty minutes in the first rack. Add onions in the second rack during last ten minutes. Remove from heat and peel and slice the beets when they are cool enough to handle. Marinate with the onions in the steam liquid for at least six hours, or overnight in the refrigerator.

Serve as an hors d'oeuvre or to accompany cold roast chicken, cold roast beef, or barbecued chicken or ribs on the deck, or at a picnic.

Steamed Buttered Beets

Serves four

1 pound small, young beets
1 tablespoon salt for steaming liquid
½ cup vinegar
Handful of fresh herbs
2 tablespoons melted butter
Parsley

Clean beets, cut off tops and roots and steam for thirty minutes over steaming liquid with salt, vinegar and herbs. When cooked, peel and slice. Serve hot with melted butter drizzled over them. Dust with finely chopped parsley.

Beets are good with a roasted chicken, lamb chops, or a leg of lamb.

Broccoli

We have already discussed broccoli in the steaming vegetable centerpiece chapter. There it was served with other vegetables and masked with lemon mustard butter sauce.

The skinniest, beautiful people will no doubt eat their broccoli with a few squeezes of fresh lemon juice and several grindings of black pepper. Broccoli is low in calories and therefore can be eaten more often and with more confidence (considering our point of view) than say, peas, potatoes and corn. Actually, few vegetables per se are high in calories, which usually add up with the addition of butter, cream and heavy sauces.

To steam broccoli, cut off the large ends, peel the remaining stems, break into flowerets and steam over salted water for eight minutes. If you include more of the stem, you'll have to steam up to twelve or fifteen minutes. By that time, however, the upper end is overcooked.

Steamed Broccoli with Sautéed Breadcrumbs and Shallots

Serves four

2 pounds broccoli
2 tablespoons salt for steam liquid
4 tablespoons butter
¼ cup minced shallots
2 tablespoons lemon juice
Salt and pepper
½ cup dried bread crumbs

In a large skillet sauté the shallots in butter, lemon juice and black pepper. When they are golden, add the bread crumbs and stir over low heat for two minutes. Add the steamed broccoli, and carefully coat the vegetable with the buttered crumbs using two wooden spoons. Delicious. This recipe is equally good with spinach and cauliflower. Try them all. Or, try broccoli and cauliflower together. A felicitous combination as you will see in the next recipe.

Steamed Broccoli and Cauliflower With Prosciutto and Parmesan

Serves six

1 head cauliflower
1 pound broccoli
2 tablespoons salt for steam liquid
2 tablespoons butter
2 tablespoons lemon juice
Salt and pepper
¼ cup finely chopped parsley
¼ pound prosciutto ham (or substitute any ham)
½ cup freshly grated Parmesan cheese

Prepare broccoli and cauliflower and steam for just five minutes over salted water. Place them on a heated ovenproof serving dish or platter. Sprinkle diced bits of butter, lemon juice, salt, pepper, half the parsley, the prosciutto and the Parmesan cheese over the broccoli and cauliflower. Toast two or three minutes under broiler. Dust remaining chopped parsley on this superior dish before serving.

This is a fine main course for lunch.

Steamed Broccoli with Crème Fraiche

Serves six

2 pounds broccoli
2 tablespoons salt for steam liquid
1 lemon
Salt and pepper
1 cup crème fraiche (or commercial sour cream)
2 tablespoons chopped pimentos

Trim broccoli, leaving about three inches of stem on the flowerets. Peel stems. Steam for eight minutes over salted water. Cut the lemon in half and squeeze over broccoli. Sprinkle with salt and then grind some pepper on it. For each serving give a good dollop of crème fraiche. A teaspoon of pimento on top of each serving adds color and piquancy.

Steamed Broccoli Vinaigrette

Steam broccoli in the usual manner for eight minutes, and serve with your own vinaigrette dressing. I use ¼ cup of the finest olive oil, 2 tablespoons lemon juice or wine vinegar, ¼ teaspoon dry mustard, salt, fresh ground pepper, 1 garlic clove squeezed through a press and 2 tablespoons chopped fresh herbs. Pour vinaigrette over broccoli just before serving. Add a lemon wedge to each plate, both for appearance, and because some like the sauce more tart.

An innovative twist is to sprinkle slivered pecans over the vegetable.

Brussel Sprouts

Brussel sprouts are a better vegetable than most people think. The standard problem is that they have been overcooked so often that they've gotten a bad name. Clean them, trim the bottom and steam them for eight to ten minutes. They should be pleasantly al dente, green, crispy and tasty.

Brussel sprouts are at their best tossed in melted butter and lemon juice with a dash of nutmeg, salt and freshly ground pepper. The following recipe is tasty and easy to prepare.

Steamed Brussel Sprouts with Ham and Cheese

Serves six

2 pounds brussel sprouts
4 tablespoons butter
1 tablespoon salt for steaming liquid
1 cup heavy cream
¼ cup freshly grated Parmesan cheese
½ cup chopped prosciutto ham
3 tablespoons dry bread crumbs
¼ cup finely chopped parsley

Steam brussel sprouts over salted water for six minutes. Drain and place on a heated, buttered serving dish. Sprinkle with prosciutto, pour on heavy cream and dust with bread crumbs and cheese. Dot remaining butter on top and half of the parsley. Pop into a 500° oven for three or four minutes until dish is bubbly and golden. Dust with remaining parsley and serve at once.

Cabbage

I've already had a spell about cabbage, so, please refer to the meals-in-one-pot section where we deal with corned beef and cabbage and you'll get the message. Loud and clear. Do not overcook. Do not permit an interesting enough vegetable to become tired and odoriferous. Cabbage is not a lofty, elegant, sensuous vegetable. It needs every bit of sensitive treatment it can get. Don't let it down. Please!

Steamed Cabbage With Bacon

Serves four

1 medium head of cabbage
¼ cup crisp bacon, crumbled
1 tablespoon salt for steaming liquid
¼ cup good olive oil
4 tablespoons lemon juice
Salt and pepper
Chopped fresh parsley

Wash cabbage and remove any tired, yellow outer leaves. Quarter cabbage and place in steamer rack over high, salted steaming water for fifteen minutes. Meanwhile, back at the skillet, heat olive oil, lemon juice, salt, pepper and parsley. Add the bacon which has been baked to crisp perfection, drained on paper towels, and crumbled.

Drain steamed cabbage, place in heated serving dish, and pour bacony vinaigrette over it. Give a final parsley dusting, and prepare to enjoy cabbage truly, maybe for the first time.

Carrots

We've discussed carrots earlier. They are excellent raw or cooked, and, like all other vegetables, should never be overcooked. If they're in strips or diagonal slices, they will steam in five minutes; if whole, a medium carrot will take about fifteen minutes. Timing varies a lot, depending upon size, freshness and age of the carrots. So, as always, *test* to make certain.

I have discovered the easiest, most effective method of cleaning carrots, if you plan to serve them whole. Don't peel, scrape or brush. Cut off stem end, steam, and when completed, just run them under warm water and the outer, dirty skin falls off with little help.

All carrots really need is to be lightly dressed with butter, perhaps a few squeezes of lemon juice, and of course, some freshly ground black pepper. Then dust with finely chopped parsley. Often sugar is added to carrots, but this is not to my taste. You can vary the herb dusting at will. Gather several fresh herbs from your yard or pots, chop them finely, and sprinkle over carrots.

Carrots are also delicious if, after steaming, they are placed in the pan juices around a roast for two minutes.

Steamed Molded Carrots

Serves four

1 cup grated carrots
¾ cup butter
1 cup flour
½ cup brown sugar
1 egg, beaten
½ teaspoon salt
1 teaspoon baking soda
1 teaspoon baking powder
1 tablespoon water
½ teaspoon lemon juice

Mix ingredients thoroughly, then spoon into a heavily greased mold. Steam over high steam for forty-five minutes. Before removing from mold place in hot oven for a few minutes. This dries surface moisture and firms the mold a bit. Let cool a few minutes and unmold.

Celery

Celery is an outstanding vegetable, more often than not eaten raw. But it also rates as a superior cooked vegetable that is simple to prepare, attractive on the plate, and an interesting variation on the menu. After all, you can get bored with all of those green beans, peas and carrots. Happily, celery is low in calories. Just eight to a large bunch.

It is also delicious when steamed and then marinated in the steaming liquid. We've created our own version of Celery Victor with this method.

Celery flavor is more pronounced when it is cooked, and is pleasantly enhanced with any of several herbs. One of the best is parsley; others I like are dill, summer savory, chervil and tarragon.

Celery is often a basic ingredient of good stocks and steaming liquids, and it frequently plays a role in many soups, stews, vegetable platters and hors d'oeuvre trays.

Basic Steamed Celery

Select a crisp, firm bunch of celery which neither looks woody and ancient, nor limp and depressing. A rule of thumb is that a large bunch of celery will serve four people. Wash it well, scrub with a vegetable brush, and shave off the outer coarse fibers with the handy little vegetable peeler we've discussed. Spread the stalks to insure the removal of all the gritty sand and dirt.

Cut the tops and leaves of the celery off about six or seven inches from the base of the stalk. Trim base carefully so that it will hold the stalks together. Quarter bunch vertically. Place over high steam for ten minutes. If quite large, you may wish to steam it a few minutes more, but don't overcook. After all, this vegetable, like so many, is eaten raw.

Lemon-buttered Celery with Fresh Herbs

Serves four

1 large bunch celery
6 tablespoons butter
3 tablespoons lemon juice
Salt and pepper
1 tablespoon each finely chopped fresh chives, chervil, oregano and tarragon

Prepare steamed celery. Melt but-

ter, add lemon juice, salt, pepper and fresh herbs. Pour over celery and serve immediately.

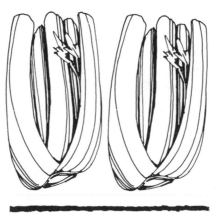

Celery au Gratin

Serves four

1 large bunch celery
6 tablespoons butter
½ cup heavy cream
Salt and pepper to taste
2 tablespoons chopped fresh dill, or one-half teaspoon dried dill
2 tablespoons dry bread or cracker crumbs
4 tablespoons grated Parmesan or Swiss cheese, or a mixture of the two

Prepare steamed celery. To melted butter add heavy cream, salt, pepper and dill. Carefully place celery quarters next to each other on an oven proof serving dish. Pour sauce over top. Dust crumbs on top and sprinkle with grated cheese. Brown under the broiler and serve while piping hot.

Steamed Celery Victory

Serves four

2 medium bunches of celery
1 quart chicken stock or 1 quart of water and 6 chicken bouillon cubes
1 cup dry white wine (California Chablis is good)
1 cup olive oil (*good* oil for better flavor)
Handful of fresh herbs—parsley, dill, oregano, tarragon, bay, etc.
4 large garlic cloves, chopped
1 teaspoon salt
12 peppercorns
2 lemons
1 tin flat anchovies
1 four-ounce jar pimentos

Combine all ingredients except celery, anchovies and pimentos in the steampot. Squeeze in lemon juice, then coarsely chop lemons and toss in. Bring to a boil and then simmer, covered, for thirty minutes. Raise heat and bring to high steam. Cut celery in quarters vertically, place in rack, and steam for ten minutes. Remove from heat, refresh celery under cold water. Strain liquid, pressing down hard on residue, and cool.

Transfer celery to a flat casserole, and add the strained, cooled cooking liquid as marinade. Cover with aluminum foil and refrigerate for five or six hours, or even all night if you have time. Handle the celery carefully so that the bunch doesn't fall apart. Tongs are helpful. Better still, before cooking, tie quartered bunches together with twine.

Remove from liquid and dust with more chopped herbs just before serving. Garnish plate with strips of flat anchovies, pimentos and a cluster of watercress. Serve as a brilliant first course.

Eggplant

I am pro-eggplant. It is an astoundingly versatile, delicious dish. It is superb grilled, broiled, fried, baked, deep-fried, you name it. It is, I find—contrary to the opinions of fine French chefs—a natural for steaming. The theory is that it needs no additional moisture and that is why you should salt it well and then drain it.

Well, I did exactly that, to concoct the following:

Eggplant à la Provençale

Serves four

2 medium eggplants
6 young scallions, chopped finely (or 1 medium dry onion, chopped finely)
1 six-ounce can tomato paste
Salt and cracked pepper to taste
Sprinkling of jalapeño sauce (or Tabasco)
Chopped parsley to garnish

Steam four salted, drained eggplant halves for fifteen minutes. Chop up the middle and add chopped scallions, tomato paste, salt and pepper and a sprinkling of jalapeño sauce on top. Place it under the broiler for three minutes, toss a handful of chopped chives on top, and you have a rather spectacular vegetable. (Of course there is moisture. After steaming, I remove the rack from the heat, turn the eggplant halves upside down, and let them drain for about three minutes before adding the tomato paste.)

Green Beans

The four common green beans we see in the market are green snap or Kentucky Wonders, sometimes known as string beans, flat Italian beans, serpentine Chinese long beans, and limas.

All should be steamed. All are delicious hot or cold. All can be served with a spartan squeeze of lemon, tossed with a tangy vinaigrette, or, served opulently with generous spoonfuls of hollandaise.

Beans combine well with other vegetables and are always a handsome addition to the plate. They can be served whole, Frenched, or in diagonally-cut pieces. (You'll recall that I look with disfavor on vegetables that have just been hacked up in hash house fashion.)

Green beans combine well with carrots, tiny white onions, mushrooms, slivered almonds, pimentos, finely chopped walnuts, tiny new potatoes, and young spring parsnips. They are the perfect vegetable with any fish, flesh or fowl.

Steaming keeps them fresh, crisp, green, tasty and healthier. Few foods are more pathetic and undesirable than green beans that have been overcooked for hours and then simply given up. They turn a dull gray, they're limp and soggy, and their once-fresh, lively taste is a thing of the past. Do not permit this in *your* kitchen.

Green Beans
á la Provençale

Serves four

1 pound Italian beans
2 tablespoons salt for steam liquid
3 ripe tomatoes, peeled
1 onion
2 large cloves garlic
4 tablespoons good olive oil
2 tablespoons fresh herbs
    (tarragon, basil, thyme,
    oregano, etc.).
Salt and pepper
2 tablespoons lemon juice

Snap ends of beans and remove
any strings. Steam fifteen minutes
or until just tender. Chop tomatoes and onion, squeeze garlic
through a press and sauté in olive
oil in a large skillet. Add chopped
fresh herbs, and salt and pepper
as desired. Cook until liquid is
thick. Add green beans, toss
quickly and sprinkle with lemon
juice.

You may wish less garlic. As Stan-
ton Delaplane of the *San Francisco Chronicle* might say,
"There's enough garlic here to
blow a safe."

This is very good with roasted
chicken, steamed pot roast or a
sizzling steak and is equally good
hot or cold.

Chinese Long Beans
Vinaigrette

These intriguing beans, sometimes a foot or more long yet
less than a quarter inch in
diameter, are quite spectacular
looking, especially when
stretched out on a platter either
hot or cold in a vinaigrette
sauce. Their flavor is commend-
able as well.

Serves six

1½ pounds Chinese long beans
1 tablespoon salt for steam liquid

Vinaigrette
¾ cup fine olive oil
3 tablespoons lemon juice or
    good vinegar
1 garlic clove, pressed
¼ teaspoon dry mustard
Salt and freshly ground pepper
2 tablespoons chopped fresh
    herbs, or 1 teaspoon mixed dry
    herbs.
2 lemons
1 pimento cut in strips

Snap off the ends of beans, wash,
and coil them in one or two
steamer racks. Cook over a full
head of steam for eight minutes or
until as tender as you like. *Don't
overcook.*

Prepare vinaigrette and pour over
beans. Serve immediately or let
them cool in the sauce and mari-

nate for several hours. Serve
them full length, or cut in half with
lemon wedges and/or strips of
pimento across them.

French Cut
Green Beans in
Mustard Lemon Butter

This is another skinny, beautiful
recipe that is as welcome an
addition to the simplest meal as to
grande cuisine from a Parisian
culinary shrine.

Serves four

1 pound Kentucky Wonder Beans
1 tablespoon salt for steam liquid
2 tablespoons butter
2 tablespoons lemon juice
½ teaspoon dry mustard
Salt and pepper
1 lemon

Snap ends and wash beans. Push
and pull through that handy little
gadget that Frenches the beans
(sometimes found on the end of a
vegetable peeler). Steam for
seven or eight minutes only since
they cook more rapidly when
Frenched. Drain. Add lemon
juice, mustard, salt and pepper to
melted butter. Drizzle over beans.
Serve with a wedge of lemon.

Steamed Lima Beans
and Shallots

For some reason I don't
understand, I seldom see fresh

lima beans either on restaurant menus or served at home. Why not? Perhaps because they are not low in calories. Nonetheless, they should be served from time to time since they are delicious in many dishes, and need only be dressed with lemon and butter. Here is a minor, tasty variation.

Serves four

2 pounds fresh lima beans
1 tablespoon salt for steam liquid
½ cup sliced shallots
2 tablespoons butter
1 tablespoon lemon juice
Salt and pepper

Shell lima beans and steam for seventeen minutes. Sauté shallots until golden in butter. Add lemon juice, salt and pepper. Toss cooked limas in this skillet or pan and serve.

Variation Prepare lima beans as above. Place in an ovenproof serving dish. Sprinkle with 4 tablespoons heavy cream, 2 tablespoons freshly grated Parmesan cheese and dust with finely chopped parsley. Brown under broiler and serve.

Variation II Prepare lima beans as above, but without the shallots. Crumble one-quarter cup bacon over beans and serve.

Leeks

Neglected and misunderstood, the leek is one of our better vegetables, and, like celery, is equally good hot or cold. Its culinary possibilities extend far beyond Vichysoisse, for which it is the noblest ingredient.

The leek is an important member of the onion family, along with chives, garlic, shallots, scallions and white, yellow and purple onions. It looks like a large, sometimes giant, scallion, but has a milder flavor.

Because the edible part of the leek is a root that is not as tightly organized as a scallion or green onion, it collects a lot of soil and sand and therefore requires extremely careful cleaning. Trim leeks so that almost no green leaves remain and, without breaking, gently spread them apart and hold them under the faucet. Better still, if you have a sink spray, use it freely, as the pressure quickly forces out every grain of dirt.

If the leeks are small, perhaps a half inch in diameter, use them whole. If larger, split lengthwise. However, the smaller ones—up to one and one-half inches diameter—are normally younger and more tender. Trim the bot-

tom, but leave enough structure to hold the leek together. For ease in handling and maintaining the attractive shape, tie enough leeks for one serving with twine, which can be removed later.

Place them on a steamer rack, and, at full steam, let them cook for seven minutes. Test with a fork to see if they are al dente, yet not raw. (I don't agree with the common cookbook recommendation to test vegetables with a sharp knife. I think the fork is more accurate, and gives us a lot more valid information.)

Remove leeks from heat. Unless you plan to sauce and serve them at once, refresh them under cold water to stop the cooking until ready to use. Who wants a limp, soggy leek?

Leeks are another vegetable that are equally good hot or cold. Skinny, beautiful people favor leeks with a simple, pristine, altogether delicious butter and lemon dressing or a perfect sauce vinaigrette. Those on the way up or down may get into a little bechamel, mornay or other sauce that may well contribute to the mature waistline. We'll deal with both points of view.

Leeks With Skinny Lemon Butter Sauce

Serves four

16 small or 8 medium leeks
1 tablespoon salt for steam liquid
4 tablespoons melted butter
Juice of half a lemon
Salt and pepper
2 tablespoons finely chopped
    parsley

Prepare leeks for cooking, tie in bundles, steam for seven minutes. Place leeks on a rectangular platter that might be used for asparagus. To melted butter add lemon juice, salt and pepper. Spoon over leeks. Garnish with finely chopped parsley.

Steamed Leeks with Crème Fraiche

Serves four

16 small or 8 medium leeks
1 tablespoon salt for steam liquid
1 cup crème fraiche (or sour
    cream)
Salt and pepper
Handful of fresh herbs, finely
    chopped (O.K. About
    one-quarter cup.)

Prepare leeks for cooking, tie in bundles, steam for seven minutes. Heat crème fraiche almost to boiling, spoon over leeks, sprinkle with salt, pepper and the fresh herbs. Serve. *Now.*

Steamed Leeks au Gratin

Serves six

12 medium leeks, split lengthwise
1 tablespoon salt for steam liquid
1 cup heavy cream
Salt and pepper
6 tablespoons grated Parmesan
    or Swiss cheese
¾ cup dry bread crumbs
3 tablespoons butter
2 tablespoons finely chopped
    parsley

Prepare leeks for cooking, tie in bundles, steam for seven minutes. Refresh under cold water. Place leeks in an ovenproof serving dish, cover with cream, salt and pepper, bread crumbs, bits of butter and grated cheese. Put under broiler for one minute to melt cheese and brown topping. Dust with finely chopped parsley.

Leeks à la Grecque

Serves six

12 medium leeks, split lengthwise
1 quart chicken stock, or one
    quart water and six chicken
    bouillon cubes
1 cup dry white wine
1 cup good olive oil
Handful of fresh herbs. Whatever
    you have is all right. Or, make a
    bouquet garni by wrapping 1
    bay leaf, ½ teaspoon dried tar-
ragon, ½ teaspoon dried
    thyme, ½ teaspoon dried
    oregano, 1 teaspoon dried
    parsley in cheesecloth.
4 large garlic cloves, chopped
1 teaspoon salt
12 peppercorns
2 lemons or ½ cup wine vinegar
6 large ripe olives
Small jar pimentos (about
    2 ounces)

Combine liquids, garlic, salt, pepper and herbs in bottom of steamer. Squeeze in the juice of the lemons, coarsely chop the rest and add. Bring to high steam. Cook leeks for five minutes. Refresh leeks under cold water and cool steam liquid. Strain liquid, pressing down hard on herbs to get all the goodies. Marinate leeks in this liquid for four or five hours, or, if there is time, overnight.

Serve bundles of leeks, strings removed, side by side on a long platter. Chop olives and pimentos, combine with one-quarter cup of marinade and pour over leeks. Dust with chopped parsley, and grind some fresh pepper on top.

This makes a delicious first course, or main vegetable with cold roasts, cold steamed salmon, or sandwiches on pita bread.

Lettuce Steam It

Lettuce is one of the vegetables

this book deals with in an un-American manner. Few of us ever eat lettuce other than raw in a salad or on a sandwich. The French, on the other hand, regard it highly as a cooked vegetable, served by itself, with other vegetables, or combined with ham, salt pork or bacon.

Naturally, lettuce when cooked will not look as crisp and fresh, but the flavor seems heightened and it is delicious. If steamed quickly, as we suggest, it retains its color. And, as with most of these recipes, it is easy to prepare.

Steamed Romaine Lettuce

Serves four

1 large head of Romaine
1 tablespoon salt for steam liquid
4 tablespoons butter
3 tablespoons lemon juice
Salt and pepper

Trim any brown or wilted outer leaves from a large, tight head of Romaine lettuce. Cut off three or four inches of the top (save for a salad or stock), and quarter, vertically. Tie each section with white string so it will hold its shape while cooking and cut after wedge is safely on serving platter. Steam in salted water five minutes. Remove from heat, drain carefully on paper towels and serve with melted butter, lemon juice

and pepper. Dust some finely chopped parsley over it. Beautiful.

Steamed Butter (Boston) Lettuce With Crème Fraiche

Serves two

1 medium head of butter lettuce
1 tablespoon salt for steam liquid
½ cup crème fraiche
2 tablespoons lemon juice
Salt and pepper
½ teaspoon dried dill, or
    1 teaspoon chopped fresh dill

Trim any wilted outer leaves. Cut in half, vertically. Tie each section with white string to hold together while cooking. Steam for three minutes. Drain on several layers of paper towels. Meanwhile, heat crème fraiche until it becomes a heavy liquid, add lemon juice, salt, pepper and dill. Pour over each wedge of lettuce.

This excellent vegetable is especially good with lamb chops, various kinds of pork, and makes a nice foil to good garlic sausage.

Steamer Special: Lettuce, Onions and Peas

Serves four

1 large head butter lettuce
2 cups shelled tender young peas
12 small white onions

1 tablespoon salt for steam liquid
Handful of fresh herbs in a cheesecloth bag. (Choose from parsley, chervil, dill, tarragon, oregano, thyme, fresh bay.)
2 garlic cloves, chopped
6 tablespoons butter
½ teaspoon sugar

To the steampot add water, fresh herbs, garlic and salt. Carefully wash lettuce, gently spreading leaves under the faucet to rinse away all sand and dirt without breaking leaves from stalk. Then cut into quarters and tie each with white string to hold shape while cooking.

Steam peas on first rack for fifteen minutes. After five minutes add onions to second rack. After five minutes more, add lettuce to third rack. Combine vegetables in a heated bowl or pot and pour the strained steam liquid over them for one minute. Stir together and then remove with slotted spoon to a serving dish or platter.

Melt butter with sugar and 2 tablespoons steam liquid, and pour over vegetables. You may wish to add a bit more salt, and some grindings of black pepper.

Onions

Onions, like celery, leeks, lettuce and certain other vegetables, are too seldom served on their own.

They are used to flavor practically anything except dessert, are tossed into soups, souffles, stews, stocks and stuffings, yet are neglected on the dinner plate.

Simply cooked, with a New England steamed dinner, they are pristine and tasty. Covered with a tangy sour cream sauce they melt in the mouth. Stuffed with fresh young peas they are exceptionally appealing. And steamed scallions or green onions are a unique, remarkably successful accompaniment to fish, chicken and chops.

The most common onion is the most potent, the yellow globe. Sweetest is the red Bermuda or Spanish onion. Most delicate is the small white onion referred to as a "boiling" onion. I hardly need remind you that *we* do not boil anything except liquid for steam.

Steamed Small White Onions in Sour Cream

Serves four

24 small white onions or 16
   slightly larger ones
1 tablespoon salt for water
2 tablespoons butter
2 tablespoons flour
1 cup sour cream
¼ cup Sauternes
Salt and white pepper
2 teaspoons Dijon mustard
Chopped parsley

Bring water and salt to high steam. Drop onions in water for one minute, remove and easily peel skins. Carefully trim so that onions don't fall apart while cooking. Place on rack and steam for seven to ten minutes, depending on size. They will be al dente, as they should be.

In a skillet melt butter, add flour, stir until smooth and cook gently for two or three minutes. Add sour cream, Sauternes, salt, pepper and mustard. Taste, and adjust seasoning if necessary. Simmer a few more minutes until thickened. Add onions, coat thoroughly with sauce, then serve, well dusted with finely chopped parsley.

Steamed Onions Stuffed With Small Peas

Serves four

4 large Bermuda onions.
2 pounds unshelled young peas
1 tablespoon salt for steam liquid
5 tablespoons butter
2 tablespoons lemon juice
Salt and pepper
Freshly grated nutmeg

Peel onions and cut off tops. Carefully scoop out all but two or three outer layers of the onion, making certain to retain a firm base. Bring water and salt to a rolling boil. Shell the peas and steam in first rack for twelve min-

utes. Add onions to second rack for the last five minutes. Fill onions with peas and steam two minutes more.

In a saucepan melt butter, stir in lemon juice, salt, pepper, and nutmeg. Spoon over onions and peas.

Serve with a steak, roast beef, leg of lamb or a roasted chicken. An attractive addition to the serving platter and dinner plate, the stuffed onions might be accompanied with tiny steamed new potatoes or julienne of carrots.

Steamed Scallions

Serves four

24 medium scallions
1 tablespoon salt for steam liquid
4 tablespoons butter
2 tablespoons lemon juice
Salt and pepper
Finely chopped parsley

Trim scallions to a length of six or seven inches. Wash carefully and trim base so that they do not fall apart. Cook over high steam for four minutes. *Do not overcook!*

Place scallions on a platter or individual serving plates, pour on melted butter, lemon juice, salt and pepper, and garnish with finely chopped parsley.

Spinach

If pressed to name my favorite vegetable, I would have to confess to a lifelong love affair with spinach. I like it in all its aspects—raw, cooked, cold, as an hors d'oeuvre, and in conjunction with pasta. I say it's spinach and I *don't* say to hell with it.

This marvelous vegetable takes a lot of loving care. Careful cleaning by soaking it in a sink or large pan full of cold water; then washing each and every leaf under running water. (Forget spinach during a drought.) You must remove every bit of sand and soil. But, there is a plus. Unless you are using it in salad, you don't have to dry it.

Steamed spinach is an important addition to the diet of skinny, beautiful people who want to stay that way without renouncing the pleasures of the palate. So hitch up your belt a notch and read on.

There's spinach and spinach, an important fact we must face. Alas, I most certainly cannot recommend New Zealand spinach, seductively packaged and crisply clean as it is. Its taste is definitely between dull and drab. There is no authoritative, assertive, fresh green flavor. The essence of spinach seems absent.

Skinny, beautiful people will have their spinach with no more than a squeeze of lemon and some freshly grated pepper. But, unless you require a totally Spartan discipline, there's not much harm in adding a little butter and sautéed shallots. If you run, ride a bike, work out, play tennis, swim or otherwise burn calories, feel free to try spinach with chopped bacon, sour cream, pasta and prosciutto, or in any one of dozens of dishes featuring this most ubiquitous vegetable.

Spinach With Shallots

Serves four

2 bunches of spinach (about
    1½ pounds)
½ cup sliced shallots
2 tablespoons butter
½ teaspoon salt
Fresh cracked pepper
1 teaspoon soy sauce
2 tablespoons lemon juice

For this recipe, we'll use a skillet, rather than the steampot we use in almost *every* other recipe. We will be steaming the spinach, nonetheless, with the water that clings to its leaves after washing.

Carefully clean spinach, removing any thick, wilted or brown stem ends. Sauté shallots in butter, salt, pepper, soy sauce and lemon juice, until they just turn golden.

Add spinach, cover for two minutes. Stir and steam one more minute. Serve at once. This is especially good with a grilled sole meunière or broiled lamb chop.

Steamed Spinach With Bacon

Serves four

2 bunches spinach (about
    1½ pounds)
4 slices crumbled, freshly baked,
    crisp bacon
3 tablespoons good olive oil
2 tablespoons lemon juice
½ teaspoon salt
Fresh cracked pepper
1 hard-steamed egg, sliced

Bacon and spinach are an excellent taste, texture and color combination. (The easiest, surest way to cook bacon well is to bake it in a pan with a rack. It cooks slowly, the grease drips away from it, and there is little danger of burning it as is so easily possible in a skillet. Drain on paper towels and keep warm.)

Heat the olive oil, lemon juice, salt and pepper in a large skillet or kettle. Add spinach, cover and steam for three minutes. Serve at once with thin slices of hard cooked egg, crumbled bacon and chopped parsley or chives.

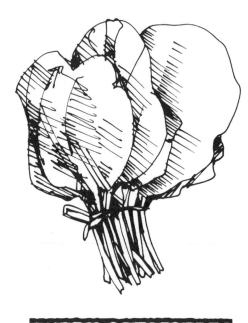

Spinach With Crème Fraiche

I hope crème fraiche is available to you. Few fruits, vegetables or meats are not enhanced by the addition of this heavy, ever-so-slightly-tart cream. Consult the chapter on basic sauces for instructions on how to produce crème fraiche in your own kitchen.

At one point I lived in the mountain ranch country of Wyoming. The beef cattle and sheep ranching families had their own milk cows, all of which produced the most incredibly heavy cream this city boy had ever seen. Before or since. Cream that could not be poured, but had to be spooned, as you would commercial sour cream. Or, crème fraiche. As my taste memory recalls, the two creams were much alike.

But I've gotten off the subject again. We're talking about spinach. The following is so simple that one can hardly call it a recipe, but it is so delicious, it would be a crime not to share it with you.

Serves four

2 bunches spinach (about
   1½ pounds)
½ cup crème fraiche
½ teaspoon salt
Fresh cracked pepper
Pinch of nutmeg

Clean spinach well, put into one of the steampot racks and sprinkle it with salt, pepper and nutmeg. Toss lightly. Cook over moderately boiling water for five minutes. Remove and drain any excess moisture, though you'll find there won't be much with the steaming method. Top each serving with a good dollop of crème fraiche and a few more passes of grated nutmeg.

Fettucine, Spinach and Chicken North Beach

This is my interpretation of a wonderful dish I have had both in Italy and just blocks away in San Francisco's North Beach, our old Italian section. Much of the city's heritage and mystique originated in North Beach. Through the years it has remained an enclave of simple trattorias, elegant Italian restaurants, fine markets, bakeries, caffès, saloons where Campari sodas and Negronis are more popular than Scotch, Martinis, and bocce ball courts. It is also the birthplace of great numbers of San Francisco politicians.

This recipe is my way of paying tribute.

Serves four

1 bunch spinach (1 pound)
1 pound fettucine, preferably
   fresh
2 cups boned cooked chicken
2 tablespoons butter
2 tablespoons grated fresh
   Parmesan cheese
3 tablespoons chopped chives
2 cups Mornay sauce:
   4 tablespoons butter
   2 tablespoons sifted flour
   2 cups hot milk
   Salt and pepper
   ¼ cup freshly grated Swiss
     cheese
   ¼ cup freshly grated Parmesan

First prepare the Mornay sauce, which is simply a creamy cheese sauce. Melt butter in a heavy saucepan, add flour and stir until it foams. Reduce heat. Gradually add warm milk and stir until the sauce thickens and bubbles appear. Add salt and pepper to taste. Off heat, gradually add the cheeses, blending well until melted. You are by no means obliged to use this half-and-half mixture of Swiss and Parmesan. You can vary this, for example, by using all one kind of cheese, or part fresh grated Romano. When sauce is ready, set aside and keep warm.

Steam spinach in first rack for three minutes, remove from heat and leave in rack to drain. (Remember, the steampot racks serve as good colanders.) Cook pasta in the steam liquid until it is al dente.

(I have successfully steamed pasta, but I have also failed. I think the best method is to toss into *large* quantities of boiling, rolling water, keep a careful eye on it, and remove it with big forks at just the right moment. It should be firm to the bite with no taste of flour. Never limp and soggy.)

Mince chicken. Add to the Mornay sauce, and then stir in the spinach. Melt the butter in an ovenproof serving dish, coating all surfaces. Toss the drained fettucine with about half of the sauce, pour into casserole, and spoon on the remaining sauce.

Sprinkle with freshly grated Parmesan cheese and dust with chives. Pop under broiler until bubbling and golden. Give a final dusting with chives, and garnish with sprigs of watercress or parsley.

This is an excellent main course, followed by a fresh green salad, lightly coated with good oil and vinegar, some fresh fruit and cheese, and a bottle of sturdy, dry white wine or a light-bodied red wine.

Squash

There was a time, back in Ohio, when I considered squash a depressing, repellant vegetable, in the same terrible class as turnips and rutabagas. One of my great-aunts served two types that still cause me to cringe. One was a whitish-green and the other was large and yellow. They were boiled and mashed into an unpleasant consistency and smelled and tasted awful.

Later, my mother served baked acorn squash that proved to be exceptionally good, and removed my antipathy about squash in general.

Today, squash is one of my favorite vegetables, providing, of course, that I do not get involved with the aforementioned yellow and white varieties.

For me, the absolute best squash is the delicious, versatile zucchini. Also good are the tiny yellow, crooked-neck summer squashes, pale green UFO-shaped patty-pans, acorn squash and the mysterious spaghetti squash. You'll not be surprised that steaming is an ideal way to cook them.

All are easy to prepare and look handsome when served. All have a unique shape, and offer creative opportunities for presentation. The zucchini and summer squash are as good raw as cooked, and must never be overcooked.

Steamed Zucchini with Mustard Butter

Serves six

6 medium zucchini
1 tablespoon salt for steam liquid
6 tablespoons butter
2 teaspoons Dijon mustard
Salt and pepper
Finely chopped parsley

Wash zucchini and cut diagonally into half-inch slices. Do not peel. Over full salty steam, cook for six minutes, or until just tender. Empty steam liquid and heat butter, mustard, salt and pepper in the hot pan. Add zucchini carefully stirring with a wooden spoon until they are coated. Transfer to a serving dish or individual dinner plates. Scatter some parsley on top.

Steamed Zucchini and Broccoli

Serves four

4 medium zucchini
1 pound broccoli
1 tablespoon salt for steam liquid
4 tablespoons butter
3 tablespoons lemon juice
¼ cup dry bread crumbs
Salt and pepper
Finely chopped parsley

Wash zucchini and cut diagonally into one-inch slices. Wash broccoli and cut away all but the flowerets and about two inches of the stem. Add salt to liquid and steam vegetables together for eight minutes. Discard liquid, add butter, lemon juice, salt, pepper and bread crumbs to pot, mix and then add vegetables. Dust with chopped parsley just before serving.

Steamed Zucchini Strips with Tomato Pepper Sauce

Serves four

4 medium zucchini
1 tablespoon salt for steam liquid
2 tomatoes
1 mild green chili pepper
Freshly chopped basil and parsley
2 tablespoons butter
4 tablespoons good olive oil
1 garlic clove, minced
¼ teaspoon sugar
Salt and pepper

Chop tomatoes, peppers, basil and parsley. Heat butter, olive oil, garlic and sugar in a skillet, add vegetables, and sauté for ten minutes.

Wash zucchini. Do not peel. Cut each into six or eight vertical strips. Steam over salted water for five minutes. Place parallel strips on a serving platter, pour on the sauce, and dust with more chopped parsley and basil.

Steamed Acorn Squash

Serves four

2 acorn squash
1 medium onion
1 tablespoon salt for steam liquid
4 tablespoons butter
2 teaspoons Worcestershire sauce
Salt and pepper
Finely chopped chives

Halve squash vertically after rinsing and scoop out seeds. Make several cross slashes on the flesh with a sharp knife. Mince onion and sprinkle on each half. Steam for thirty minutes covered, over full steam.

Remove from heat, pour off any water, and with a fork, mash the surface. Add one tablespoon butter, ½ teaspoon Worcestershire sauce, salt and ground pepper to each, and mash into squash. Dust with chopped chives before serving.

Steamed Spaghetti Squash Alfredo

One of nature's mysteries was revealed to me just a few years ago. I suppose it has always been around, but I had never heard of spaghetti squash. At a dinner party, something resembling an orange-yellow honeydew melon appeared at the table. Ho hum. But then the hostess took a few jabs at it with a fork and in an instant it was transformed into what appeared to be genuine, no-nonsense, real spaghetti. The hostess then proceeded to heat butter in a hot chafing dish, and with large wooden forks, gently mixed in the "spaghetti." She ground generous amounts of aged Parmesan cheese into it and lots of good black pepper. Finally, she dusted the incredible vegetable-pasta with finely chopped chives.

It was completely delicious, tasted remarkably like pasta, yet was lower in calories. And, it was great tabletop theater. Sometimes called string squash, I only see it in the markets during the summer.

Serves six

1 medium spaghetti squash
2 tablespoons salt for steam liquid
½ cup butter
½ cup grated Parmesan cheese
3 tablespoons chopped chives
Salt
Coarse ground pepper

Do not peel squash. Cut into quarters. Steam on two racks of the steampot for thirty-five minutes, or until, at the test of a fork, the squash starts to shred. Don't overcook. In a chafing dish at the table, heat butter and toss spaghetti squash (which you have shredded easily, with a fork, from the rind) with it. Then grind or sprinkle on the cheese, and add salt and lots of freshly ground black pepper. Sprinkle liberally with the chives. It can be offered as a first course, as you might serve fettucine, or with the main meal. Dramatically, pick up the pieces of squash, jab with a fork, and 'ecco'—spaghetti!

Steamed Tomato Cups With Peas

Serves four

4 large firm tomatoes
2 pounds shelled peas
1 tablespoon salt for steaming liquid
4 tablespoons butter
Salt and pepper
4 teaspoons finely chopped fresh oregano

Cut a wide top off each tomato. With a spoon, carefully remove pulp and seeds from center. Melt butter, add salt, pepper and chopped oregano, and coat insides of each tomato cup. Fill each with peas and steam for ten minutes. Carefully remove the fragile cups and serve at once.

Tomatoes à la Provençale

Serves six

6 large, firm tomatoes
1 tablespoon salt for steaming liquid
2 cloves garlic
½ cup chopped parsley
½ cup dried bread crumbs
½ cup good olive oil
Salt and pepper

Cut off upper third of tomatoes. Shake carefully to remove seeds and excess liquid. Steam for five minutes. Meanwhile, sautè finely chopped garlic, parsley and bread crumbs in oil. Season with salt and pepper. Spoon mixture over tomatoes just before serving. Grind more pepper over each.

STEAMY FRUIT FRONTIERS

Steam and fruits were made for each other. Moist heat enhances flavors, preserves colors, and, of course, does not wash away the nutrients. Not only do fruits make an outstanding dessert, they're great served with meat, fish and fowl.

Since most fruits can be steamed so successfully, when you serve them, what you combine with them and how you present them is limited only by your imagination. Creative cookery and presentation are what this book is about. Don't be timid.

What could be more effective and unusual than bunches of green grapes served with a leg of lamb? Or steamed peaches or pears with a crown roast of pork? Or wedges of fresh pineapple with a thick ham steak? Or a dried fruit compote with a steamed or roasted chicken?

Desserts can be as simple as rhubarb garnished with mint. Or as lavish as an apple with heavy cream, Cointreau, butter and cinnamon. Or as totally delicious as a pear with ice cream and chocolate sauce.

Au Cointreau, Sir— Steamed Apples
Serves four

4 large, crisp, firm apples (Jonathan, Rome Beauty, Winesap or Pippin are best. Avoid mushy textures.)
¾ cup heavy cream
6 tablespoons Cointreau (or Triple Sec, Calvados or good Port)
2 tablespoons butter
4 pinches cinnamon
2 tablespoons brown sugar

Wash apples and cut an extra-large hollow in the middle of each with an apple corer, leaving enough of the base so liquid will not run out. Steam for ten min-

utes. Remove apples and drain any collected moisture. To each add one teaspoon butter, one teaspoon brown sugar and cream almost to the top of each well. Carefully add Cointreau. Sprinkle liberally with cinnamon. Place in steamer again for ten minutes.

Heat one-quarter cup heavy cream and two tablespoons Cointreau and pour over each apple just before serving. Serve with small, simple cookies.

Skinny Steamed Apples
Serves two

2 large, crisp apples
2 tablespoons honey
2 tablespoons lemon juice
2 pinches cinnamon

Wash apples, core almost through, but leave a base. Add honey and lemon juice to each. Sprinkle with cinnamon. Steam for twenty minutes.

Steamed Apple Breakfast Slices

Serves four

4 crisp apples
4 tablespoons butter
4 tablespoons brown sugar

Wash apples, core, and cut off each end. Cut into three or four thick slices. Place in two steamer racks. Steam seven minutes. Place on cookie sheet or large pan or dish, coat with a mixture of melted butter and sugar. Pop under broiler for one minute.

Serve overlapping slices on heated platter with crisp bacon, link sausages, and scrambled eggs. Great combination of flavors!

Steamed Apples, Sausages and Applesauce

Serves six

6 crisp, tart apples
2 tablespoons brown sugar
½ teaspoon cinnamon
2 tablespoons butter
12 French, Italian or English
    sausages (Bangers)

Wash and core three of the apples, cut off ends, and cut each into four slices. Peel and core the other three apples, cut in small pieces and place in a bowl or cas-serole that will fit into the steamer rack. Add one tablespoon sugar and the cinnamon. In another steamer rack, place the apple slices. Steam both racks over high steam for ten minutes. Remove and mash the apples in the bowl into sauce. (You may wish to steam a few minutes more.)

Presentation Grill the sausages until golden brown. Spread applesauce on a heated oven-proof platter or flat casserole serving dish. Make a neat, symmetrical arrangement of sausages in the middle of the platter. Overlap the apple slices around these. Melt the remaining tablespoon of butter, mix with brown sugar and coat the apple slices.

This is a wonderful brunch dish, served with warm croissants and brioches with sweet butter, and, as a festive addition, champagne, or one of California's excellent sparkling wines.

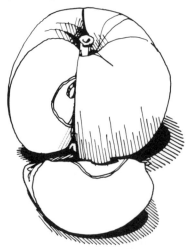

Flaming Steamed Stuffed Apples

Serves four

4 crisp apples
¼ cup chopped walnuts or
    pecans
¼ cup apricot jam
2 tablespoons butter
½ cup brandy or Bourbon
Core apples almost through, but leave a base. With a sharp knife, carefully cut a large, cone-shaped opening to make the well. Add equal parts of nuts, jam and butter to each. Steam for twenty minutes.

Bring to table on a serving dish. Heat brandy or bourbon in a metal butter melter or flame-proof bowl, ignite and ladle over apples.

Flaming Steamed Bananas in Rum

Serves four

4 ripe bananas
4 tablespoons butter
½ cup brown sugar
4 tablespoons shredded coconut
½ teaspoon nutmeg
½ cup rum

Do not peel bananas before steaming, but jab several holes in them with a fork to allow steam to escape. Steam them over high steam for seven minutes. Because the steamed bananas are fragile, remove half of the skin by splitting it along each side with a sharp knife and peeling it back.

Just before time to serve dessert, heat the butter in a chafing dish or large, flat skillet, and add sugar, coconut and nutmeg. Control heat so sugar doesn't burn. Stir well. Carefully lift bananas and place peeled-side-down into skillet, and lift off remainder of skin. Slick, easy and it works. Spoon the coconut butter sauce over bananas, and squeeze half a lemon over each. Pour pre-warmed rum (brandy if you prefer, but the rum is great) over bananas and ignite. Serve at once.

Steamed Fresh Fruit Compote

Serves six

3 apricots
3 plums
3 peaches
½ pound Bing cherries
2 tablespoons vanilla extract
1 cup sugar
4 cups water

Cut apricots, plums and peaches in half and remove stems. Pit cherries. Add sugar and vanilla to water and use as steam liquid. Steam fruits in rack for ten min-

utes. Remove from heat, place fruit in liquid and steep for thirty minutes. Put combined fruits in dessert dishes. (I don't have any so I use large wine glasses, or some sturdy, round beer glasses with stems. You could also use those flat, wide-mouthed champagne glasses. They are certainly not good for champagne, since they are designed so that most of it will slosh out.)

Cook the remaining syrup over high heat for a few minutes to thicken it, and then spoon over the fruits. A bit of kirsch or Cointreau is not bad, either.

Grapes

Unlikely as it steams, grapes are a delicious accompaniment to various meats, chicken, and fish. Green seedless grapes are best.

Steam bunches of them for ten minutes and serve them with lamb-legs, racks, crown roasts and chops. They are also quite good with a crown roast of pork. And what could be better than a moist roasted chicken with chestnut stuffing, beautifully garnished with clusters of green grapes?

For dessert, try steamed grapes dusted with powdered sugar and served with crisp little cookies.

Steamed Grapes to Accompany Meats and Poultry

Serves four

1 pound Thompson green seedless grapes
4 tablespoons juices from meat or poultry

Wash grapes, leaving them on stems, and cut into four bunches. Steam for ten minutes. Place on serving platter with meat, and spoon natural juices over grapes.

Steamed Frosted Grapes

Steam grapes for ten minutes, then dust with powdered sugar. For heavier frosting, dip grapes into eggwhite before sugaring.

Peaches

Peaches are another simple, but great dessert and fine companion to meats and poultry. Of course they are delicious raw, as are most fruits and vegetables, but there are times when a steamed peach becomes an important culinary event. Try a steamed peach with raspberry sauce and créme Chantilly. Or a simple steamed peach in wine. Or halves of steamed peaches with thick ham slices.

Wine-steamed Peaches
Serves four

4 ripe peaches
2 cups California red wine.
   Zinfandel is excellent.
2 tablespoons sugar

Heat wine and sugar in steamer.
Add whole unpeeled peaches to
rack. Steam eight minutes. Remove from heat and peel with a
sharp knife, then marinate
peaches in liquid for thirty minutes. Cut in half, remove pits. Reduce steam liquid over high heat
to half its volume. Spoon over
peaches.

This recipe is similar to that for
pears steamed in wine, although
we have substituted red for white
wine. Actually, either could be
used for either fruit.

Steamed Peaches in Raspberry Sauce
Serves four

4 ripe peaches, preferably White
   Babcocks
4 tablespoons granulated sugar
3 tablespoons vanilla extract
4 cups water
1 pint fresh raspberries
2 tablespoons powdered sugar
½ cup heavy cream
1 tablespoon Cointreau or Kirsch

Peel, halve and pit peaches. Add
granulated sugar and two tablespoons of the vanilla extract to
four cups of water, and heat in
steampot. Steam peaches twelve
to fifteen minutes or until just tender. (An al dente peach?) Transfer
peaches to liquid and refrigerate.
Purée the raspberries through a
sieve. It's worth the effort. A
blender will, unfortunately, blend
the rather bitter seeds along with
the raspberry pulp. Add one of
the tablespoons of powdered
sugar and the Cointreau and
steam together. Cover and refrigerate.

To the heavy cream add the remaining tablespoons of powdered
sugar and vanilla, and whip until it
just begins to hold peaks. Don't
overwhip the cream. I think it
loses some of its character and
taste.

Serve peaches in individual glasses or bowls, cover with raspberry
sauce, and ring with whipped
cream. (Highly recommended
variation: Add a heaping tablespoon of fresh blueberries to each
glass. Exceptional and lovely!)

Pears

The first thing to bear in mind
when cooking pears is that they
should be quite firm. I do not use
Bartletts because they often seem
too ripe, and are not really suita-
ble for cooking. Comice pears
may be the most attractive to
serve, with their handsome, long
shape. If pears are small, such as
the delectable little green-brown
Winter Nelis, use two per person.
A pair of pears.

As you know, I am anti-peeling.
But in this case I think the pear
should be peeled for purely aes-
thetic reasons. Use that handy little floating blade gadget I have
mentioned, the vegetable peeler.
It removes the thinnest layer of
peel, and easily glides along the
shape of the fruit. Knives require
far more alertness. Be sure to
leave the stem on.

Steamed Pears in Heavy Cream

Serves four

4 large pears, preferably Anjou, Bosc, Comice or Winter Nelis
1 cup freshly whipped cream
2 tablespoons brown sugar
4 tablespoons Cointreau or Eau de Vie à la Poire William (pear brandy)
Cinnamon

Start with clean water for your steaming liquid. Get up a full head of steam, place the pears on the rack just above it, and steam for five minutes.

Carefully remove, place on plate, spoon the beautifully nuanced whipped cream over the pears, and dust with cinnamon. (Nutmeg is great, too.) A neat touch is to put a sprig of mint under the stem.

Wine Steamed Pears

One of my favorite desserts is the most simple of all to prepare, pears steamed in white wine. You'll enjoy this fine dessert with a fraction of the calories of pastries or mousses. Dessert, after all, should not be the culinary straw that breaks the camel's back, but a pleasant postscript. A good night kiss. A happy wrap-up.

Serves four

4 large pears. Preferably Comice. They look better.
2 cups good Sauternes
2 tablespoons brown sugar

Heat Sauternes and sugar in steamer kettle. Add pears to rack. Steam five minutes. Remove from heat. Reduce steam stock over high heat to about half its volume. Pour over pears just before serving.

Pear Today, Gone Tomorrow

Serves two

2 firm ripe pears
½ pint vanilla ice cream
6 ounces melted bittersweet chocolate

Peel pears. Carefully core from the bottom leaving pears intact and retaining the stems. Cut a thin slice from bottom so pears will stand up. Steam for eight minutes. Cool and chill. Soften ice cream and coat the pears, following their shape. Put into freezer for ten minutes. Heat chocolate until it is syrupy. Hold pears by stems and immerse them in chocolate. Put back in freezer for a few minutes before serving. The idea is to have firm chocolate and ice cream, but not to freeze the pear. Garnish with a couple of mint leaves by pear stems.

For a variation, bring pears with ice cream and mint garnish to table, and pass a sauceboat of chocolate.

Pears Belle Hélène. Sort of.

Serves four

4 firm pears
1 cup honey
3 cups water
1 tablespoon vanilla extract
1 pint vanilla ice cream
4 ounces bittersweet chocolate
½ cup sour cream

Peel pears, carefully core from bottom, leaving pear intact with stem. Steam-poach on first rack for ten minutes over water, honey and vanilla. Remove from heat and cool pears in liquid. Be sure to rotate pears or baste them several times. Chill in refrigerator, not freezer.

Melt chocolate with sour cream. Whip until smooth. Spread slightly softened ice cream in a serving dish. Stand pears in ice cream, and pour chocolate sauce over all.

An interesting garnish would be the elegant, thin little jelly candy mint leaves.

EGGSPERIMENT WITH STEAM

Why we haven't been steaming eggs right along I do not know. It is an ideal way to control the delicate egg, keep it tender, in shape, and properly cooked all with the utmost ease.

There are many variables in egg cookery, above all, the egg's state of freshness. Practically any other food reveals something of its condition simply by looking at it. Not so the eggcentric, secretive egg. For, until the shell is broken, we don't have the faintest idea about its quality. Even then, all the facts are not known until we start to cook it.

One important rule to remember: Do not cook eggs straight from the refrigerator. If you want them to cooperate, they should always be at room temperature.

Out of curiosity, I experimented with lots of eggs. (Remember, we're concerned with cooking as a creative experience. Just as in painting, though you know the basics about color, form, line, shape, texture, edges and sur-

faces, it is not until you start moving paint around the canvas that you know what the possibilities are. It is the same in cooking. We know basic facts about food and equipment, but until we move beyond the obvious, we do not become creative cooks.)

The eggsperiment was successful! Eggs can be soft-steamed, hard-steamed, steam poached, shirred and scrambled. Furthermore, the major problem of poaching enough eggs for four or more people and serving them all at the same time is easily overcome.

Especially interesting are steamed soufflés. They puff beautifully, retain a moist texture and are delicious. I pop them under the broiler for thirty seconds to get a handsome, toasted golden finish.

Also highly successful are steamed eggs on corned or roast beef hash. For an unusually appealing dish, dust the steamed eggs and hash with grated Parmesan cheese, and pop this under the broiler for one minute. Terrific!

57

Hard and Soft Steamed Eggs

Place eggs directly on steamer rack, over high steam. For soft-cooked, which approximates a typical "three-minute" egg, steam for five minutes.

For hard-cooked eggs, steam for fifteen minutes. Take from the heat and plunge eggs into cold water so the shell can be easily removed.

Steamed Poached Eggs

Lightly butter small ramekins, individual quiche or tart dishes, or whatever ceramic, china or glass dishes will be the correct size to hold two eggs neatly. Break two eggs in each dish. Place dishes on steamer rack over high steam. Cover. Cook three minutes and serve at once.

Scrambled Eggs

Serves four

10 fresh eggs
⅓ cup cream
4 drops Tabasco sauce or 1 teaspoon green chili or jalapeño sauce or 1 teaspoon Worcestershire sauce
Salt and pepper

Break the eggs into a bowl and beat well. Add the cream, one of the sauces, and the salt and pep-

per. Place bowl on rack over high steam. Cover. In three minutes stir eggs, and stir again every two minutes. Steam a total of twelve minutes. Serve on a hot platter. Dust with finely chopped parsley.

Don't overcook the eggs. Even if you prefer them rather well cooked, remember, they continue cooking even after they have been removed from heat. And if the platter is quite warm, I allow for this as a factor too.

Shirred Eggs

2 eggs
2 tablespoons butter
2 tablespoons heavy cream
½ teaspoon chopped chives
Dash of Tabasco sauce
Pinch of dried dill
Salt and pepper

Place individual ramekins or dishes in the steamer rack and

melt one tablespoon butter in each. Break two eggs into each dish. Combine remaining ingredients except for chives and pour over eggs. Place in steamer rack over high steam and steam for six minutes. Garnish with chopped chives.

Steamed Souffles

Frankly, what are souffles except a lot of puffed up hot air? Empty bubbles wrapped in cheese or spinach or whatever. Air today, gone tomorrow.

Well, in our steam laboratory we have come up with a new type of souffle. Moist, delicious and with a firmer grip on the filling. It starts out in a puffed, expansive manner, but once removed from the steam, settles into a no-nonsense, richly-textured consistency. Then, you pop it under the broiler for a few minutes and it majestically reasserts itself while toasting.

All of which means, I confess, that steaming souffles is an interesting experiment, but with results that may not please every souffle aficionado. But they are quite tasty, moist, and perhaps as related to quiche as to a souffle.

Steaming souffles is possibly the most adventuresome of our eggsperiments.

Steamed Tuna Souffle and Switzerland Cheese

Serves four

4 egg yolks
5 egg whites
3½ tablespoons butter
3 tablespoons flour
1 cup milk
1 cup canned tuna (water packed)
½ cup freshly grated Switzerland cheese
2 tablespoons chopped fresh herbs (a good combination is chives, dill and parsley.)
Dash of Tabasco sauce
Pinch of nutmeg
Salt and pepper to taste.

Melt 3 tablespoons of butter then gradually stir in flour. Bring to a boil, stirring constantly, then remove from heat. Beat egg yolks with 2 tablespoons of milk. Stir into flour mixture. Add Tabasco, nutmeg, herbs, salt and pepper. Stir in cheese and tuna. Keep warm over low heat.

Beat egg whites until they stand up in firm peaks, then carefully fold into tuna cheese sauce.

With the remaining butter, grease a 1½ quart souffle dish. Pour in mixture and place on first steamer rack over medium steam. Cover and cook for 25 minutes. Remove from steam. (Don't panic. It will fall.) Place under broiler for a few minutes, or until souffle has puffed up again, and is toasted golden and brown. Serve at once.

Steamed Eggs and Corned Beef Hash

Serves four

4 eggs
2 cups finely chopped corned beef or roast beef
½ cup finely chopped onion
4 medium potatoes, pre-steamed for twenty-five minutes and diced
3 tablespoons butter
Dash Tabasco sauce
1 teaspoon Worcestershire sauce
Salt and pepper

You *can* use corned beef or roast beef hash available in cans. But it is so much better if you cook your own. And simple.

Sauté the onion in a skillet with the butter, and add the Tabasco, Worcestershire sauce and salt and pepper to taste. Then add the potatoes and meat.

Place the hash in a medium-sized casserole or baking dish that will fit inside a steamer rack. With a cup or the back of a large spoon, make four wells, where you'll drop the eggs. Steam hash five minutes, remove from heat. (If water collects in wells, just pour it off.) Carefully drop eggs in hollows. The safest way to do this is to break them into a bowl, one at a time, and slip into the well. Add one tablespoon light cream to each egg, dust with a pinch of dried dill, and steam three minutes more, or until eggs are cooked to your liking. Remove from steamer, dry bottom of casserole and serve at table. Eggsquisite!

59

BREAD, ROLLS AND MUFFINS: TASTEFUL, WELLBREAD STEAMING

Who needs steamed bread? Only our endless quest for creative cookery has driven me to steaming bread. Result? Excellent, in many instances. Disasters? A few.

Steaming dough is hardly unique. The Chinese steam rolls. Many cuisines offer steamed dumplings. And, of course plum puddings and numerous variations on the theme are steamed into culinary masterpieces.

Sadly, I am not a baker, for I've never taken the time to delve into this seemingly mysterious art. Those chemical formulas. Those rigid parameters. I rely heavily on the packaged pre-mixes, if indeed I bake at all. So, forgive me if I speak readily of Bisquick, Duncan Hines Blueberry Muffin Mix, or Dromedary Cornbread Mix. I'm sure other brands are just as effective. They are not from scratch, but I *can* do them. And they produce esteamable results.

Joy Windle, my eagle-eyed editor, has probably never used a mix, culinary purist that she is, and she informs me that recipes from scratch produce equally laudable results. In this section we include her recipe for French rolls, which all seem to agree, acquire particularly lovely texture and glazed crust from the steaming process.

No-Crumble Steamed Corn Muffins

Eight muffins

Follow directions on an eight-ounce package of corn muffin mix, taking care to mix lightly so batter is still lumpy. Grease muffin pan cups or use paper baking cups. Fill two-thirds full. Place in steamer rack with full steam up. Cover, steam fifteen minutes.

Remove from steamer. Let muffins cool in pan for five minutes and remove. Brush with butter, pop under broiler for one minute for a golden toasting.

The steam muffins rise in uniformly perfect round domes. The texture is light, yet not crumbly so that the muffins disintegrate when you butter them, as so often happens with baked muffins. Naturally, steaming cannot brown the breads, but a fleeting moment under the broiler does the job, yet retains the moist steamed quality.

Small muffin pans will fit into the steamer rack. If yours is too large, use individual metal or Pyrex cups.

Steamed Blueberry Nut Bread

Grease and flour a 9″ × 5″ × 3″ loaf pan. Use one package prepared blueberry muffin mix. In this case, we've used Duncan Hines. Open tin of blueberries, empty into a strainer and wash under cold water. Set aside to drain.

In a bowl prepare muffin mix according to instructions on package. Mix until well blended, then gently fold in blueberries. Spread batter in the loaf pan. Place on rack over full steam for forty-five minutes. Remove from heat and let stand ten minutes before removing bread from loaf pan. Brush with butter and brown for three minutes in a 500° oven.

Idalene Allman's Steamed Zucchini Bread

⅔ cup oil
1 cup sugar
2 eggs beaten
1½ cups grated zucchini (about two medium zucchini)
¾ teaspoon grated lemon peel (The yellow zest only, not the white part. The same applies to orange peel.)
¾ teaspoon grated orange peel
2 scant cups sifted flour
¾ teaspoon salt
½ teaspoon cinnamon
Pinch cardamom
¼ teaspoon ginger

¼ teaspoon nutmeg
¾ teaspoon baking soda
1½ teaspoons baking powder
½ cup chopped walnuts
1 teaspoon vanilla

Add oil and sugar to the eggs and beat well. Coarsely grate unpeeled zucchini, lemon and orange peel, add to mixture and beat well. Sift flour and all dry ingredients together and add. Stir in chopped walnuts and one teaspoon vanilla. Spoon into a buttered nine-inch by five-inch loaf pan. Place on steamer rack over high steam. Cover, of course.

Steam for one hour. (Be certain you have lots of water in the pot.)

Cool in the pan until easy to remove. Brush with melted butter.

Pop into hot oven for four or five minutes, to firm surface, then cool on a wire rack.

French Rolls à la vapeur

2½ cups warm water (105°- 115°)
1 package dry yeast
1 tablespoon salt
7 cups unbleached flour
  (approximately)

Dissolve yeast in warm water. Add the salt and four cups of flour and mix with the hands. Add more flour half a cup at a time until dough leaves the sides of the bowl.

At this point turn the dough out onto a well-floured surface and knead until smooth and elastic, about eight minutes. Place in a clean greased bowl and let rise until double in bulk at a temperature of 85°. This will take about one and one-half hours.

Shape into either round or long rolls and place in two or three steamer racks, leaving room between the rolls for expansion. Steam for fifteen minutes, then place on a baking sheet and brown in a 350° oven for another ten minutes.

Though it's hard to imagine improving on something as wonderful as traditional French bread, if you're bold enough to try this, I wager you'll be more than favorably impressed.

STANLEY STEAMER'S HOLIDAY DINNER FOR SIX

Cold artichokes, stuffed with bay shrimp

Turkey

Chestnut and wild rice stuffing

Tender, young, slim buttered carrots

Green and wax beans

Miniature onions

Pots de crème à la vanille

Espresso

Heitz Cellars
Cabernet Sauvignon
1968

Chandon
Napa Valley Brut

My friend Stanley is too modest to have his entire name mentioned, but he is one hell of a steam chef. Perverse, too. He would never serve turkey on Thanksgiving or Christmas, but featured it at his recent Easter dinner party. It may well have been the most tender, moist, delicious turkey I have ever eaten. Remarkably, it was steamed. In fact, the entire meal was steamed, from hors d'oeuvre to dessert. It was not strange. It was wonderful.

The Stanley Steamer Holiday Dinner

Serves six

The artichokes stuffed with fine little bay shrimp were served cold as the first course, on artichoke plates with a well for sauce, and an area around the perimeter where leaves are stacked with painterly concern, after the good part has been eaten. The sauce was a lemony mayonnaise. The shrimp were the freshly boiled variety available in better markets. A light sprinkling of dill on top was just right.

The wild rice and chestnuts were steamed together for the same length of time. Then the chestnuts were ground in a blender, mixed with the rice and made into stuffing for the turkey.

The stuffed turkey was steamed in the top level of the steamer, where the high-domed lid fit with room to spare.

When it was nearly cooked, the carrots were placed in the middle level of the steamer, soon followed by the green and wax beans, and finally the small onions.

Before the guests arrived, Stanley had already steamed the luscious pots de crème à la vanille, and chilled them for our hardly-needed, yet much-enjoyed, dessert.

Artichokes—Select six artichokes with good green color and petals tightly closed. Avoid those with spots and dried outer leaves. Cut stem off flat at bottom and trim neatly with a scissors. Rub all cut areas with half a lemon to keep from turning black.

To two quarts of water, add three tablespoons olive oil, four or five coarsely chopped cloves of garlic, a dozen peppercorns, the juice of one lemon, and the rinds. Steam for forty minutes. Chill. Gently spread leaves and remove chokes. Stuff with fresh bay shrimp and a healthy dollop of homemade mayonnaise.

Turkey—Stanley's bird weighed 11 pounds, 10 ounces before it was stuffed. It was clearly a young, fresh fowl, and not the type that pops buttons out when cooked. After stuffing and trussing he steamed it for one and one-half hours. (A meat thermometer in the breast will help.) The steaming liquid was one bottle of California Pinot Chardonnay, and two cups of chicken stock. Twice he added a cup of water to the stock. After steaming, he coated the turkey with butter and soy sauce and lightly glazed it for ten minutes in a 375° oven.

Chestnut and wild rice stuffing

½ pound wild rice
¼ pound dried chestnuts
  (available in Italian markets)
1 cup butter
2 bunches scallions
1 celery heart with the leaves
Salt and pepper
1 teaspoon poultry seasoning

Place a layer of cheesecloth over the steamer rack. Carefully wash rice and place it and the chestnuts on the rack. Steam over water for three and one-half hours. When cool, grind about two-thirds of the chestnuts in a blender or food processor. Chop the rest.

Sauté the scallions and celery in the butter. Add salt, pepper and seasonings, then the wild rice and chestnuts. It is now ready to be used as stuffing.

After the turkey has been steamed and is glazing in the oven, cook the vegetables, using the same steaming stock.

Carrots—Select tender, young carrots, preferably elegantly slim ones. If they are large, cut them lengthwise into half inch strips. Steam twenty minutes.

Green and wax beans— Add another rack while the carrots are steaming. Steam the beans about fifteen minutes. Select them carefully. Avoid those that are curled or wilted. Pick the straightest, most handsome ones in the bin. If you want to French them, steam them for just ten minutes.

Small onions—These are the white boiling onions that are tender and delicious. Pop them

into boiling water for one minute and the skins can be easily removed. Steam them for eight minutes.

Pots de crème à la vanille

2 cups whipping cream
½ cup sugar
pinch salt
6 egg yolks
1½ teaspoons vanilla extract or
    1 inch vanilla bean

Stanley often serves this delicious dessert, sometimes varying it with chocolate. It is much easier to cook it in the steamer than by the usual method of placing the cups in a pan of hot water in the oven. Just scald cream with sugar until melted. If using vanilla bean, scald with cream and sugar, then scrape out the seeds. Beat egg yolks thoroughly, and then pour hot mixture over them, beating constantly. Add pinch of salt and vanilla extract. Pour into pots de

crème or custard cups. (If the latter are used, cover tightly with foil.) Steam for thirty-five minutes over medium steam or until knife inserted shows it to be gently solid. Chill well.

To serve Serve the artichokes first. After the plates have been removed, serve the turkey on a heated platter, surrounded by watercress. Watercress, my favorite garnish, is much less common than parsley. However, I am much in favor of finely chopped parsley dusted over vegetables, meats, eggs, fish and fowl. An excellent variation, both for taste and appearance, are chopped chives.

Serve the vegetables on another heated platter, with carrots in the center, and neat parallel bundles of beans on either side. At one end, mound the onions. Drizzle lemon butter over the platter, dust chopped parsley over the onions, and then sprinkle a band of chopped parsley straight across the beans/carrots/beans.

The pots de crème à la vanille are small and should be served (in the pot) on a small dessert plate, with a couple of sinfully rich, expensive cookies. Bake them if you can, and if you know how (I do not!), or get them at your finest bakery.

Clockwise from center: William Gaylord, Thea Michaels, Peter Galvin , Katie Murphy, Chris Luke, Susan Galvin. Photo taken in William Gaylord's apartment.

THE MISTY ASSIGNATION DINNER FOR TWO

Champagne   Dom Perignon

Blue Point Oysters on the Half Shell

Seductive Sole
Steamed with bay shrimps, scallops and sorrel,
masked with Sauce Mousseline

Snow Peas
Steamed with butter and lemon

Watercress and Hearts of Palm
Walnut Oil Vinaigrette

Stemmed Strawberries, Dipped in Chocolate

Champagne   Dom Perignon

Victoria Rathbun and Juan Rosendo

People who steam together *seem* together, as I've often said. With this in mind, Joy Windle and I created The Misty Assignation Dinner for a couple whose turbulent liaison was again heated up over a steampot. All of us are convinced that this menu rates ten on a scale of ten for aphrodisiac qualities.

Further, it is low in calories, high in energy and a cinch to help you become beautiful, skinny and successful. At least in the kitchen. It is also quite delicious.

The Dom Perignon is a tantalizing way to start the evening, a no-nonsense, clear-cut statement about the nature of the event. But the oysters, whose properties are known to every school boy, really structure the plot and establish interesting parameters.

Seductive sole tantalizes. Provokes. Excites. It's a palate teaser: an absolute pleaser. The snow peas are a crisp counterpoint, a cautionary note to hang in there. After all, dinner is still in progress.

The watercress and hearts of palm salad are a bridge, a pause, an opportunity for reflection, a falling back and regrouping, a quiet opportunity for strategic planning.

Poets have said that chocolate may well be the most sensuous, most arousing of all foods, an exquisite brown velvet caress. Wrapped around long stemmed strawberries, the dessert becomes the ultimate, the definitive expression of culinary passion.

More Dom Perignon, softer lights and wistful music. Now it's up to you.

Seductive Sole

Serves two

2 large or 4 small fillets of sole
¼ cup bay shrimp
4 scallops
½ bunch sorrel
Salt and pepper
Sauce Mousseline
2 tablespoons grated Parmesan
  cheese

Steam sorrel for four minutes. Remove and chop. Steam scallops for three minutes. Mince finely. Spread shrimp, scallops and sorrel on sole, sprinkle with salt and pepper and roll. This may be prepared a couple of hours in advance and refrigerated.

When ready to eat, steam sole for five minutes, mask with Sauce Mousseline, sprinkle with Parmesan cheese and glaze under the broiler until brown.

Sauce Mousseline

1 egg yolk
1 tablespoon lemon juice
⅓ cup melted butter
Salt
¼ cup heavy cream

Whip the cream and set aside. Mix egg yolk with lemon juice and set in a metal bowl in the top of the steamer. Gradually add melted butter and blend with a wire whisk until the sauce thickens. Add salt. Fold in whipped cream.

SAUCES: HOW TO TOP YOUR OWN COOKING

Sauces are rather personal, I think. Of course there are standard recipes, but infinite variations can reflect your taste, your mood, the availability of ingredients, and your attitude about an interesting combination a certain sauce and meat, or sauce and fruit, for example, might create.

As you know, if you're really determined to be skinny and beautiful, your sauces will necessarily be Spartan. A squeeze of lemon and a few grindings of pepper on vegetables and meats. A squeeze of lemon and perhaps some finely chopped mint on fruits. Perhaps a small dollop of sour cream on vegetables, meat or fruit. (Spartan or not, the results can be terrific!)

Fair enough. But, if you are not leading too sedentary a life, you can move onto a light vinaigrette; a simple lemon, butter and mustard sauce; more sour cream, mustard and herbs; and for desserts, heavy cream, brown sugar, lemon and a good splash of Cointreau or brandy.

One of my favorites, you will have noted in preceding pages, is crème fraiche, a seductive, delicious, heavy cream that has been mysteriously uplifted. Crème fraiche goes anywhere. Spoon it over asparagus. Fold it into some fresh peas. Mask a meat pie. Ladle it over an elegant steamed pear. Slather it right on top of Idalene Allman's wondrous apple, nut and date bread. Dip a strawberry into it and sing Hallelujah.

So, in our usual, no pressure manner, we'll pass on a few simple recipes for each of these sauces, confident that you, creative chef that you are, will consider them as suggestions, and certainly not as serious rules.

Vinaigrette

This is the most simple sauce of all, perfect for salads and vegetables, and quite good with chicken, fish and some meats as well. It is composed, simply, of oil, vinegar, salt and pepper. The oil should be top quality olive oil, wondrous walnut oil, or perhaps a vegetable oil. The vinegar can be of any of several types; perhaps you may prefer lemon juice. You can even try grapefruit or orange juice, as I have in emergencies, and have been intrigued with the results.

Simply stir ingredients together, shake them in a jar, or perhaps blend them briefly in the electric appliance. I use the great little plastic gadget, with two, tightly fitting halves, each with an indented base, that is a perfect shaker for the vinaigrette and many sauces.

For ½ cup

6 tablespoons oil
2 tablespoons vinegar
1 teaspoon salt
½ teaspoon freshly ground
    pepper

A good idea is to let the salt dissolve first in the vinegar, then add the oil and pepper.

Variations include the oils and juices we have suggested, and naturally, the embellishment of whatever herbs you may have in your garden, and the authority of garlic in well-considered quantities.

Butter/Lemon/ Mustard Sauce

Most vegetables respond to a simple butter/lemon/mustard sauce. Artichokes, snow peas, spinach, carrots, zucchini and potatoes come to mind. As do cabbage, broccoli, cauliflower, green beans, corn on the cob and steamed lettuce.

You really don't need a recipe, although one follows. Just melt butter (if you're watching your cholesterol, use margarine, I think the results are fine), drizzle in some lemon juice, briskly stir in Dijon mustard, grind some good fresh black pepper on top, and you've got a great sauce. Sometimes I stir in dry Colman's Mustard rather than the prepared Dijon type.

For ½ cup

6 tablespoons butter
1 tablespoon Dijon mustard
1 tablespoon lemon juice
½ teaspoon salt
½ teaspoon fresh ground pepper

Into softened butter, whip mustard, lemon juice, salt and pepper. Spoon dollops over meats, vegetables, meat pies and eggs.

Sour Cream/ Mustard/Herbs

This sauce is equally good made with sour cream, heavy cream or crème fraiche. You simply add mustard, pepper and lemon juice and serve with most vegetables and meats. Without mustard, herbs and butter, and perhaps with a bit of sugar, it is perfect for fruits and hot pastries.

For ½ cup

½ cup commercial sour cream
1 tablespoon Dijon mustard (or 1
    teaspoon Colman's dry
    mustard)

74

Handful of finely chopped fresh
  herbs (Parsley, tarragon,
  thyme, oregano, bay, basil,
  summer savory, or whatever
  you have.)
1 teaspoon lemon juice or vinegar
½ teaspoon salt
½ teaspoon freshly ground
  pepper

Whip all ingredients together and
spoon, with an elegant flourish,
over practically anything. Within
reason.

Crème Fraiche/Herbs

A few years ago I discovered
crème fraiche. It does not pour,
but is spooned, and in fact, can be
cut with a knife. Crème fraiche is
the cousin to American super
heavy cream, the likes of which
few of us have ever seen. It is very
French. It is absolutely great.

Apparently, I gather from my
French friends, crème fraiche,
heavy to begin with, is allowed to
mature, and at some point, begins

to ferment, and to assume a
unique, almost nutty flavor. If you
live in San Francisco, New York,
or a few other privileged cities,
you can probably buy crème
fraiche. If not, do not despair.
Here I am, your friendly tramp
steamer, to help. To reveal the
mysteries; to take you over the
rainbow to a sublime experience:
to crème fraiche.

Follow a cow until you obtain one
cup of heavy cream. If you're not
up to all of that, buy a cup of
"whipping cream." Add 1 teaspoon of buttermilk. Stir. Heat it
gently, slowly, perhaps in your
steamer, until it is lukewarm,
about 85-90 degrees on a thermometer. Pour the mixture into a
glass bowl or large cup, cool to
room temperature, and let stand
until it thickens. In warm weather
it will thicken more rapidly than in
cooler temperatures.

It stands alone. But it is also a
good mixer. For desserts add
sugar, nutmeg, cinnamon, vanilla,
lemon juice and chopped mint.
For vegetables add fresh herbs,
Tabasco, pepper, green peppercorns and garlic.

Crème fraiche should always be
in your refrigerator. Ready for
Frenched green beans. Available
for asparagus. Waiting for strawberries. Sturdy enough for bollito
misto. The ultimate accolade for

tarts and puddings. A sauce for all
seasons.

Cointreau Cream

This is another simple,
uncomplicated sauce that is
delicious. It is simply sweetened
heavy cream, whipped or not,
with a splash of lemon juice and
vanilla, perked up with Cointreau,
Triple Sec, brandy or other
liqueur. Variations include
nuances of nutmeg, cinnamon,
finely chopped mint, grated
coconut, chopped nuts, raisins
and shaved bittersweet chocolate.
Use it on steamed fruits
(sometimes spoon it into apples,
pears and peaches while they are
steaming), on cakes, desserts
such as plum pudding, and over
fresh strawberries, blueberries,
raspberries or ripe figs.

For a generous ½ cup

1 cup whipping or heavy cream
1 tablespoon brown sugar
2 tablespoons Cointreau or other
  liqueur
½ teaspoon vanilla
1 tablespoon lemon juice

Briskly stir ingredients together
and serve as is, or add any of the
variations suggested above. If you
prefer to whip the cream, do so
first, then fold in other ingredients.

DESSERTS: PUDDING THEM IN THE STEAMPOT

Steamed fruits are great desserts of course, and we've dealt with them at length in the section on fruits. Some of the steamed breads, such as blueberry nut and zucchini, are superb desserts if topped with whipped, sour or heavy cream, or the highly special Crème fraiche. In the chapter about Stanley Steamer's Holiday Dinner, we've used a recipe for Pots de Crème à la vanille.

Puddings, custards and mousses are naturals for the steamer. (Traditionally the pots of dessert are placed in pans of boiling water.) The steamer provides consistent, even heat, and is a lot less bother than dealing with pans of water.

Here, we'll consider three lush and opulent steamed desserts that are not, sadly, an option for many people who wish to remain skinny and beautiful. However, if you jog, cycle, swim and successfully burn excess calories, whatever the method, read on.

First there is Joy Windle's private family recipe for plum pudding, a dessert of such lofty importance that whenever it is served, the event becomes an occasion for celebration. Then she dazzles us, seductively lures us onto a culinary Valhalla, with her chocolate hazelnut rum cake. Finally, we wrap up with Idalene Allman's apple date nut pudding, an achievement of significance, a steamed dream.

Chocolate Hazlenut Rum Cake

Serves twelve

6 ounces semi-sweet chocolate
¾ cups sweet butter
¾ cup sugar
6 eggs, separated
1 cup ground, toasted hazlenuts
1 tablespoon dark rum

Butter a nine-inch cake pan. Melt chocolate and rum in the top of the steamer. Let cool. Cream the butter and sugar. Add egg yolks one at a time and blend thoroughly. Stir in the chocolate and hazlenuts. Beat the egg whites until stiff and fold into the chocolate mixture. Pour into the prepared pan, cover with foil and steam for an hour. Let cool in pan before removing. When thoroughly cooled, ice and chill before serving.

Chocolate Frosting

1/3 cup heavy cream
6 ounces semi-sweet chocolate
1 tablespoon dark rum
2 tablespoons softened sweet butter

Melt chocolate with cream in top of steamer. Add rum. When cool, beat in softened butter and spread over cake.

Joy Windle's Family Plum Pudding

Serves eight

1/3 cup ground blanched almonds
⅞ cup dry breadcrumbs
1 cup minced suet
1 cup brown sugar
½ teaspoon salt
½ teaspoon cinnamon
½ teaspoon nutmeg
½ teaspoon cloves
1 cup currents
1/3 cup raisins
2 tablespoons candied lemon peel
1 cup heavy cream
1 egg + 1 egg yolk
2 tablespoons rosewater
¼ cup cognac

Mix almonds, breadcrumbs, suet, sugar, salt and spices. Add currants, raisins and lemon peel. Next add cream, well-beaten eggs, rosewater and cognac and mix thoroughly.

Pour into a greased, one quart mold with a tight-fitting lid or cover securely with aluminum foil. Steam three and three quarter hours or until set. To unmold, set into cold water, and when loosened, invert onto serving dish.

Garnish with a sprig of holly and serve with hard sauce. For additional drama, heat more cognac, pour it over the pudding and serve it flambé.

Idalene Allman's Steamed Apple Date Pudding

Serves eight

This is a delicious, rich dessert, not unlike a plum pudding. In fact, hard sauce is a good accompaniment. Easier, and just as tasty is heavy cream, heated, laced with brandy or Cointreau and spooned over the wedges of pudding or cake.

For one 9" diameter cake pan

2 cups chopped apples
½ cup chopped dates
¼ cup raisins
½ cup chopped walnuts
¼ cup oil
1 egg, well beaten
1 teaspoon vanilla
1 cup unsifted flour
1 cup sugar
½ teaspoon salt
1 teaspoon baking soda
½ teaspoon cinnamon

Mix apples, dates, raisins, walnuts, oil, egg and vanilla together. Combine flour, sugar, baking soda, salt and cinnamon and then add to the apple mixture. Mix well. Pour into loaf pan and place on rack over high steam, covered, for one hour.

Cool until loaf can be easily removed from pan. Brush with melted butter and place in a hot oven for four or five minutes. Cool on a wire rack.

Index of Recipes

BREAD

Blueberry Nut Bread 62
French Rolls à la Vapeur 63
Idalene Allman's Steamed Zucchini Bread 62
No-Crumble Corn Muffins 62

DESSERTS

Au Cointreau, Sir, Steamed Apples 51
Chocolate Hazelnut Rum Cake 78
Chocolate Frosting 78
Flaming Bananas in Rum 52
Flaming Stuffed Apples 52
Fresh Fruit Compote 53
Idalene Allman's Apple-Date Pudding 79
Peaches in Raspberry Sauce 55
Pears Belle Hélène, Sort of, 55
Pears in Heavy Cream 56
Pear Today, Gone Tomorrow 55
Plum Pudding 78
Pots de Crème à la Vanille 67
Stemmed Strawberries Dipped in Chocolate 71
Wine Steamed Peaches 54
Wine Steamed Pears 55

EGGS

Eggs and Corned Beef Hash 59
Hard and Soft Steamed Eggs 58
Scrambled Eggs 58
Shirred Eggs 58
Soufflés 59
Steamed Poached Eggs 58
Tuna and Switzerland Cheese Soufflé 59

FRUIT

Apples 51
    Au Cointreau, Sir, 51
    Breakfast Slices 52
Flaming Stuffed Apples 51
    Skinny Steamed Apples 51
    with Sausage and Applesauce 52
Bananas 52
    Flamed in Rum 52
Fresh Fruit Compote 53
Grapes 53
    to Accompany Meats and Poultry 53
    Frosted Grapes 53
Peaches 53
    in Raspberry Sauce 54
    Wine Steamed 54
Pears 54
    in Heavy Cream 54
    Pears Belle Hélène, Sort of, 55
    Pear Today, Gone Tomorrow 55
    Wine Steamed 55
Strawberries Dipped in Chocolate 71

MEAT

Bollito Misto 9
Choucroute Garni 11
Corned Beef and Cabbage 13
Couscous 15
Pot au Feu and Poule au Pot 10
Steamed Apples, Sausages and Applesauce 52
Steamed Eggs and Corned Beef Hash 59

POULTRY

Chicken Babylon 16
Couscous 15
Fettucini, Spinach and Chicken North Beach 46
Poule au Pot 10
Steamed Chicken, Herbs and Vegetables 17
Turkey with Chestnut and Wild Rice Stuffing 66

SAUCES

Butter/Lemon/Mustard Sauce 74, 31
Cointreau Cream 75
Crème Fraiche/Herbs 75
Lemon/Dill Butter 25
Sauce Mousseline 71
Sour Cream/Mustard/Herbs 74, 10
Vinaigrette 74, 40

VEGETABLES

Cold Vegetable Spectacular 30
Openers and Hors d'oeuvres 30
Steaming Vegetable Centerpiece 31
Artichokes 32
    Stuffed with Bay Shrimp 66
Asparagus 33
Beets 34
    Cold Beets Vinaigrette 34
    Steamed Buttered Beets 34
Bell Peppers 31
Broccoli 34, 31
    with Sautéed Breadcrumbs and Shallots 35
    and Cauliflower with Proscuitto and Parmesan 35
    Vinaigrette 36
    and Zucchini 48
Brussels Sprouts
    with Ham and Cheese 36
Cabbage 36
    with Bacon 36
Carrots 37, 66
    Steamed Molded Carrots 37
Cauliflower 31
    and Broccoli with Proscuitto and Parmesan 35
Celery 37
    Lemon Buttered with Fresh Herbs 38
    au Gratin 38
    Steamed Celery Victory 38
Cherry Tomatoes 31
Eggplant 39
    à la Provençal 39
Green Beans 39
    à la Provençal 40
    and Wax Beans 67
    Chinese Long Beans Vinaigrette 40
    French Cut in Mustard/Lemon/Butter 40
    Lima Beans and Shallots 41
Leeks 41
    with Skinny Lemon Butter Sauce 42
    with Crème Fraiche 42
    au Gratin 42
    à la Greque 42

Lettuce 42
    Steamed Romaine 43
    Butter Lettuce with Crème Fraiche 43
    Lettuce, Onions and Peas 44
Lima Beans with Shallots 41
Onions 43, 31
    White Onions in Sour Cream 44
    Stuffed with Small Peas 44
    Scallions 44
    Small Onions 67
    Potatoes 31
Snow Peas 31
Spinach 44
    with Shallots 45
    with Bacon 45
    with Crème Fraiche 46
    Fettucini, Spinach and Chicken North Beach 46
Squash 47
    Acorn Squash 48
    Spaghetti Squash Alfredo 49
    Zucchini 31
    Zucchini and Broccoli 48
    Zucchini with Mustard Butter 47
    Zucchini with Tomato Pepper Sauce 48
Tomatoes 49
    à la Provençal 49
    Cherry Tomatoes 31
    Tomato Cups with Small Peas 49

SEAFOOD

Artichokes Stuffed with Bay Shrimp 66
Chilled Steamed Salmon 25
Crab and Asparagus au Gratin 24
Crab with Artichoke Hearts 24
Mary Ri's Steamed Seafood Soiree 20
Paella 14
Salmon Steaks in Dill 25
Seductive Sole 71
Steamed Crab, Prawns and Clams 24
Steamed Curried Clams 23
Steamed Dungeness Crab 24
Steamed Oysters à la Provençal 22
Steamed Seafood Stew 22

NOTES

OTHER BOOKS BY TAYLOR & NG:

PLANTCRAFT By Janet Cox. A practical and fun guide to indoor plant care. Illustrated charts depict the growing characteristics and conditions for over 60 plant varieties. Photo gallery by L.C. Spaulding Taylor.

HERBCRAFT by Violet Schafer. The mystery of herbs unveiled: 87 pages describe 26 herbs—their origin, history, use, growing and storing conditions. Illustrated by Win Ng.

COFFEE. The story behind your morning cup: Charles & Violet Schafer elaborate on coffee—its origin, many varieties, how to brew it and what to brew it in. With recipes for companion foods. Illustrations and photography by Alan Wood.

CHINESE VILLAGE COOKBOOK. Authoress Rhoda Yee tells her story—all about the wok and wok cookery, coupled with colorful narratives on everyday life in a Chinese village. A stir fry chart, photographic food glossary and authentic recipes guide the novice to wok mastery in no time!

DR. TERRI McGINNIS' DOG & CAT GOOD FOOD BOOK. Authoress Terri McGinnis, veterinarian and pet expert, unravels fact from fiction in this up to date, clear, concise, and convenient guide to pet nutrition: what to look for in commercial foods, how to cook up your own at home, how to recognize and feed special needs. Illustrated by Margaret Choi.

DIM SUM. Rhoda Yee teaches how to prepare a Chinese Tea Lunch at home! Explicit recipes for preparing the traditional delicasies with a chapter on suggested menus make *dim sum* easy and exciting to do. Photographic.

GREAT ASIA STEAMBOOK by Irene Wong. The first compendium of the steam-cooking techniques and recipes of all Asia. Includes dishes from Japan, China, Thailand, the Phillipines, Tahiti, Vietnam, Hawaii, Korea and Indonesia. Photos by Nadine Ohara.

WOKCRAFT by Charles & Violet Schafer. An authoritative and entertaining book on the art of Chinese wok cookery. Authentic, easy to follow recipes for beginners and professionals alike. Illustrated by Win Ng.

RICECRAFT. Authoress Margaret Gin delves into the fact, fiction and fancy of rice. A collection of inventive recipes takes full advantage of the international versatility of rice. Fanciful illustrations by Win Ng.

TEACRAFT—a treasury of romance, rituals, and recipes. A book of tea—its multiplicity of uses and varieties, how to test and taste, plus recipes to complement teatime. Written by Charles & Violet Schafer, illustrated by Win Ng.

BREADCRAFT by Charles & Violet Schafer. A connoisseur's collection of bread recipes: what bread is, how you make it, and how you can create your own bread style. Plus a chapter devoted to breadspreads! Illustrated by Barney Wan.